FINDING NEW SYMBOLS

WWW.HADEANPRESS.COM

FINDING NEW SYMBOLS

Cath Thompson

For Jim

CONTENTS

FOREWORD

THE TITLE OF this book is taken from *Liber AL* Chapter II verse 55, "Thou shalt obtain the order & value of the English Alphabet; thou shalt find new symbols to attribute them unto." The magickal order and value of the English Alphabet, predicted by Dr John Dee, unwittingly encoded by Aleister Crowley, and sensed by Austin Osman Spare, was obtained by James Lees in 1976. The English Qaballa provides a portrait of reality in which numeric symbols are used to correlate the observably manifest with the intuitively perceived. New attributions of the 26 English letters have been discovered using the Complete Tree of AL II:76 as a template; 12 Zodiac Signs, 10 planets, and 4 Elements, plus the individual's Inner Self, and the Eternal Source, have their expressions in this cosmology, which enables a technique of divination by English Qaballistic methods. This is an account of how this was accomplished, and of some of the consequences.

I must thank Erzebet and Dis for their enduring good humour and patience.

.

PART ONE

A QUESTION OF APPLICATION

WE KNEW THAT the English Qaballa had been used as a tool in the conjuring of spirits in the tradition and style of the ancient grimoires. We wondered whether the techniques and procedures of the goetic magician would be effective in the evocation and invocation of spirits hitherto unlooked for and undiscovered in the English Qaballistic system. It seemed a reasonable proposition, and we undertook the project and agreed an astrologically suitable date to begin.

PROPOSAL

The 28 characters of AL II:76 are Keys by which it is possible to contact certain spirits that are inherent within Liber AL .

EXPERIMENT

1. To prove the Proposal, by constructing Tables of Correspondences.

2. To prove the Tables by using them to construct Rites of Invocation.

3. To prove the invocations by performance in order to contact the hypothetical 28 Spirits and obtain their Names and Sigils.

4. To prove the existence of the 28 Spirits by repeated performance of the invocations, and investigation of their individual rank, characteristics, and abilities.

The Complete Tree of Life, or Two Tree system, delineated in *Liber Al* Chapter II verse 76, should be familiar to students of the English Qaballa. At the moment it is enough to remind the reader of the twenty-eight character sequence of letters and numbers given in AL II:76, "4,6,3,8,A,B,K,2,4,A,L,G,M,O,R,3,Y,X,24,89,R, P,S,T,O,V,A,L;" referred to here as the 28 Key Graphemes.

II:76 shows a continuous cycle which neither begins at Manifest Malkuth and climbs arduously to the top, nor starts at Unmanifest Kether and spreads radiantly downwards. Although either interpretation is entirely possible and plausible, a third reading (which is in accordance with the Creation described in *Liber AL*) has its inception at the central "O" of the 93 section.

Referring to Diagram 1 on page 14, what we might call the event of Creation, or the pulse of light, or the start of an out-breath, may be easily visualized as originating from the "O" and passing at once to the M=21 and the R=12 on either side. Note the symmetry of the numbers 21, 12 flanking the empty circle, illustrating the Creation process described in AL I:28, "None, breathed the Light... and Two."

Pairing off the Graphemes of AL II:76 we find that the perfected Malkuth/Da'ath and the X of the 93 section are arrived at simultaneously, followed by the Manifested Kether and the Cosmic Yesod, which gives some insight into how the perfection of the Cosmic Tree occurs, and what the reflection of the Divine Countenance is looking at.

Continuing up the Cosmic Tree and down the Tree of Manifestation we find that there are relationships between the Sphere of Chokmah in Manifestation and the Cosmic Hod, where the purest logic of Heaven informs the manifestation of the Principle of Force; and we see the beauteous Netzach in Heaven communicating the Supernal Form of Binah on Earth. The architecture of the Divine Plan in Manifested Chesed is delineated by the Perfected Tiphareth. The Manifest and the Unmanifest Geburah coincide, indicating that energy discovers energy. Then the Sphere of Chesed in Heaven determines the harmony of Tiphareth in Manifestation, the Cosmic Binah bringing forth the Goddess in Manifest Netzach, and Chokmah Unmanifest delineates the force of Intellect in the Manifest Sphere of Hod. Yesodic Manifestation is informed by the Heavenly Kether; and the Sphere of Malkuth in Manifestation is where the sequence turns around and begins to withdraw back to the central "O'" again.

Incidentally, we can ascribe the quarters of the Lunar cycle to the 28 Spheres as follows. The empty circle of the central "O" is the Dark of the Moon, and the Full Moon is attributed to the "L" of the Manifest Malkuth. The Light or Energy then expands and contracts symmetrically as described above. The first and last gibbous stages fall at the Cosmic and Manifest spheres of Geburah. We cannot however precisely map the Lunar cycle onto II:76, for it only averages 28 days, and sometimes lasts longer than 29 days.

This composite symbol is the template upon which we based our correspondences, as required in the first step of our project. For the greater clarity of a detailed examination, which is our present intention, the first seven Spheres of the 93 section, the "trunk" of the Complete

Tree, are presented horizontally left to right, while the final "X" remains immediately above Kether on the Tree of Manifestation. This pattern, less tree-like but reminiscent of many illustrations of a three-plane model, will provide Kabbalists with a representation of the three "Veils of Negative Existence" beyond Kether; it reveals a lot more besides, as we will demonstrate later on.

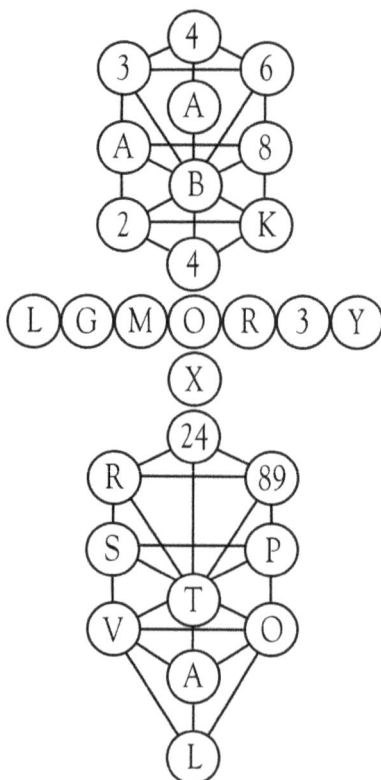

DIAGRAM 1: THE COMPLETE TREE OF LIFE.

FINDING NEW SYMBOLS

To begin with, we found that the text of *Liber AL* furnished us with twenty-eight Names, which opened a range of possibilities for Lunar and other ritual purposes, duly exploited in order to ratify our interpretation. These Names are, in order of appearance in the text: Had, Nuit, Hadit, Aiwass, Hoor-paar-kraat, Khabs, Khu, Khonsu, Ra-Hoor-Khu-it, Asar, Isa, Nu, Heru-pa-kraath, Tahuti, Ra-Hoor-Khu, Ra Hoor Khut, Hrumachis, Heru-ra-ha, Mentu, Ra, Ka, Tum, Khephra, Ahathoor, Bes-na-Maut, Ta-Nech, Jesus, Coph Nia. We omit the alternative spelling of Hoor-pa-kraat, and leave aside names such as Mary and Mohammed as having too much mortal about them. We find this reasoning justifies the absence of the scribe's full name, Ankh-af-na-Khonsu, from our list but permits the inclusion of the god-name which is part of the scribe's rank or title.

One can see that a number of these Names correspond by E. Qaballistic evaluation with traditional symbols. NUIT=FIRE for example, HADIT=LIBRA and TAHUTI=SCORPIO. After some time and effort it became clear that each Name belonged to a particular Sphere of II:76, and that through a synthesis of Western Occult Revivalist correspondences with the English Qaballistic model, the symbolism of the Tarot was also attributable. We bowed our heads to the inevitable and drew up a Table.

The Tarot as it was handed down to us has 22 Major Arcana, comprising the symbols of the 12 Zodiac Signs, 7 planets, and 3 Elements. We expanded this symbol set to include the three outer planets which were (it seems) unknown to the ancients. We then saw that we had to include our own planet, Earth. The fourth Element exists in its own terms in this system. Our Table then completed itself with the symbol of Spirit understood as Infinite Consciousness or Universal Spirit-Mind-Life, and the symbol of Self understood as a quantum of spiritual existence or an individually conscious singularity, composed of pure Will.

The Table below shows the Key Grapheme of AL II:76, the attributed Name, and the new Symbol, of each of the 28. These attributions took over a year to prove, by ritual, meditation, and divination concentrated on every decision. During the process other discoveries were made, quite unexpectedly expanding the area of study and experiment.

KEY Grapheme	SYMBOL	NAME
4	PISCES	RA HOOR KHUT
6	FIRE	NUIT
3	WATER	TA NECH
8	CAPRICORN	BES NA MAUT
A	ARIES	RA HOOR KHUIT
B	SPIRIT	JESUS
K	TAURUS	AHATHOOR

2	AIR	RA
4	GEMINI	HOOR PAAR KRAAT
A	NEPTUNE	HERU PA KRAATH

L	AQUARIUS	KA
G	LEO	HRUMACHIS
M	SCORPIO	TAHUTI
O	LIBRA	HADIT
R	VIRGO	ISA
3	CANCER	KHEPHRA
Y	SAGITTARIUS	ASAR
X	WILL	KHU/HOOR

24	URANUS	HAD
89	PLUTO	HERU RA HA
R	SATURN	RA HOOR KHU
P	JUPITER	MENTU
S	MARS	KHABS
T	SUN	NU
O	VENUS	COPH NIA

V	MERCURY	AIWASS
A	MOON	KHONSU
L	EARTH	TUM

TABULATED CORRESPONDENCES OF II:76, SYMBOLIC ELEMENTS,
AND NAMES IN LIBER AL

In the following explanation of this table we keep to the order of the old Hebrew-letter Tarot for convenience, but the reader will find a number of new attributions which may be confusing to begin with. Familiarity with the model of the Complete Tree of Life delineated by AL II:76 will no doubt assist in clarification of this system, which is actually quite coherent and consistent, possessing a pleasing symmetry, and harmonising with standard Hebrew Kabbalistic dogma as taught in Western Occult Traditionalism. (See Diagram 2 on page 31).

0. The Air element and the character of The Fool is ascribed to RA, one of the earliest names of the Sun Gods. Ra has a myriad of different forms and additional names and titles, like different identities that he carries as he travels about the skies, in the same way that the Fool has all his characters in his sack. Placed in Unmanifest Hod, the mobile and active nature of Air is balanced by the placid firmness of Taurus in Unmanifest Netzach. The attributed Key Grapheme of II:76 is the symbol-number 2, the number of division and duality.

1. AIWASS is identified with the planet Mercury. *Liber AL* tells us that Aiwass is the "minister of Hoor Paar Kraat" where HOOR PAAR KRAAT = GEMINI, the Zodiac

Sign traditionally ruled by Mercury. V is the Key letter, the 26th Grapheme of II:76, the shape suggesting the raised invoking arms of the ritualist, and also the focus of analysis, and the central point, and so on. Corresponding with Hod in Manifestation, Aiwass is balanced by the attribution of COPH NIA (=88=MASTER) to Manifest Netzach.

2. KHONSU is identified with the Moon and therefore with The High Priestess. KHONSU=56=ISIS. This is the penultimate Key of II:76; its Grapheme is A=1=ONE=WOMAN. 56 is also the value of FEAR, revealing a relationship with the 5th Grapheme in Unmanifest Geburah and the 27th, Yesod in Manifestation, both of which again repeat the letter "A" as their Grapheme.

3. COPH NIA, whose force is called double-wanded, is identified with the planet Venus and The Empress, and the 25th Grapheme of AL II:76, which as we have remarked is the Sphere of Netzach in Manifestation. The Key letter-symbol is O, a clear echo of the central O in the 93 section, where the symbol LIBRA is traditionally ruled by Venus; and is amplified by the value of the Name COPH NIA=88=CIRCLE. Her sacred animal, the Cow, is reflected in the Unmanifested Netzach and its symbol TAURUS which is also ruled by Venus.

4. Aries, the Zodiac sign most closely associated with Horus the Avenger and activities of war and vengeance, is ascribed to The Emperor and to RA-HOOR-KHUIT. Placed in Unmanifest Geburah, the Cardinal Sign of Spring is balanced by the Cardinal Sign of Winter (Capricorn) in Unmanifest Chesed, the Perfected Plan of Creation: both Zodiac Signs are symbolic of birth. AL II:76 gives the letter-symbol A for the fifth Key.

5. Taurus is ascribed to Unmanifest Netzach and the mystery of The Hierophant, the animal in question being in this case more in the nature of Hathor's Cow than the Earth Bull. The Key Grapheme is the letter K=9, and NINE=76=TAURUS. It appears to be the least dynamic of all the first ten Keys – but 9 is the number of the Sphere of Illusion, and the letter K is associated with the Kundalini chakra: attributions that serve to lift the symbolism out of the heavy solidity of the earth and illuminate the Woman on The Hierophant card in the Thoth pack. This added buoyancy is present in the balance across the Heavenly Tree with the Unmanifested Hod and its symbol, Air. The Name is that of the Egyptian form of Venus mentioned in *Liber AL*, AHATHOOR.

6. Gemini has the same E. Qaballistic value as HOOR-PAAR-KRAAT=117 and THE LIGHT, a number which corresponds with the Manifested Kether when the Key Graphemes are studied in conjunction with 93. We have already noted that Aiwass, the minister of Hoor-paar-kraat, is the Name attributed to the symbol of Mercury – who is the planetary ruler of Gemini. But this is the 9th Key of II:76 and so Hoor-Paar-Kraat and the symbol of Gemini (the Lovers) are accordingly ascribed to Unmanifest Yesod, where they may be thought of in this context as corresponding to that Light which is beyond the Veils of Inexpressibility.

7. The armour of the Beetle, KHEPHRA, is an easy match with that of the warrior in the Chariot, the creature itself sharing characteristics with the Cancerian Crab. The Key Grapheme is the number 3, which also appears in the Unmanifest Binah; the resonance is with concepts of motherhood, (Cancer being the House of the Mother) of forming, of stability, and PEACE=THREE.

8. HADIT=58 has the same E. Qaballistic value as LIBRA, whose association is always with Justice. It is the perfect balance of the infinitely tiny particle. 58 is also the sum total of all the first ten Keys of AL II:76, indicating the non-spatial perfection of Unmanifestation (or Heaven). The Name is ascribed to the 14th Key of II:76, the central O of the 93 section and the symbol from which Manifestation occurs. The O is a symbol of perfection – with an inclination to become imperfect, an impossible necessity framed in 93.

9. ISA is easily ascribed to Virgo. The Key Grapheme of II:76 is the letter-symbol R, whose shape is part of the symbol of Virgo. There is a further relationship with the repetition of the letter as the 21st Key Grapheme of the Manifest Binah, for She is the Mother of Sorrows as personified by the Goddess Isis (ISA) who walks alone and veiled; thus embodying the character of the Hermit.

10. MENTU, who seems to have been one of the earliest hawk-headed gods, is depicted with the ostrich plumes of Maat on his crown and is associated with promulgating laws of morality; his correspondence therefore is with Jupiter and with Chesed in Manifestation. MENTU = 101 = ACHIEVE, DISCOVER, DIVINE, ELEVEN, is a numeric formula of Change and thus attributable to the Wheel of Fortune; the Formula of "Solve et Coagula" in the Perfected Chesed is the informing influence. This ordered activity is balanced across the Manifest Tree by the raw energy of KHABS=39=MARS.

11. HRUMACHIS stands out somewhat in the list as an unusual spelling of the Greek translation of the Name of the Child-god, who, seated upon a Lotus flower with finger on lips, suggests silence and is perhaps being playful.

Associated with Leo which is the astrological House of the Child, the value of the Name is 100 = LITTLE, DAUGHTER, and QUEEN. The Key Grapheme is G, an oddly inscribed G in the scribe's handwriting, with a second bar above the usual horizontal termination of the bottom curve of the letter: the shape suggests an opening (or a closing) of a mouth, the action of the Woman traditionally depicted in the Strength card.

12. TA-NECH has the same E. Qaballistic value as TRUTH and CHRIST and is associated with the Element of Water by the context in AL III:38, "...by wise Ta-Nech I weave my spell," where WATER=65=WISDOM and SPELLS. The Sephirotic correspondence is with the Unmanifest Binah, where the balance is with the Element of Fire (FIRE=78=NUIT) in the Unmanifest Chokmah; and the Supernal Triad in Heaven is completed by NOTHING=PISCES=RA HOOR KHUT=97. Ta-Nech was the name of Ankh-af-na-Khonsu's mother; here we see the relationship between the Key of this Sphere and that of the 16th, which share the number 3; for the latter is ascribed to Cancer which astrologically speaking is a Water Sign and rules the Home and the Mother.

13. TAHUTI has the same E. Qaballistic value as Scorpio. Generally thought of as a male Moon-god, (only possible under 93), he is credited with the knowledge of the correct pronunciation of Words of Power – including those sounds employed to raise the dead – and indeed 93 is the value of LISTEN and the anagram SILENT. The association with Death needs no elaboration. The Key Grapheme in AL II:76 is the letter-symbol M in the 93 section of the sequence, part of the MOR complex by which manifestation is accomplished.

14. ASAR is ascribed to Sagittarius and the Art Tarot card, as befits a deity of Life-in-Death; an appreciation of the 418 Formula may be necessary to harmonise this correspondence, where SAGITTARIUS=HEREAFTER is what comes after Death (SCORPIO). The Key Grapheme is the letter-symbol Y, a triangulation of three into one; the E. Qaballistic value is 15, 3x5, and as 5=S it is suggestive of three wave-forms of energy in different dimensions, or of three bends in space at right angles to one another. Incidentally, the pronunciation of the letter is the same as the word WHY=22, the value of X, the next Key Grapheme on the way to (and from) Manifestation

15. BES-NA-MAUT has the same E. Qaballistic value as BAPHOMET and is therefore matched with Capricorn, the Devil of the Tarot. It is placed in the Unmanifest Sephirah of Jupiter where its curiously composite divinity is balanced across the Cosmic Tree with the Babe of Aries. As Lord of the Zodiac, Capricorn stands apart somewhat as an emblem of perfect authority; hence the attribution to the Perfected Chesed and the 4th Key Grapheme of II:76. This is the symbol-number 8, whose shape is also a symbol of infinity.

16. KHABS has the same E. Qaballistic value as Mars, and is placed in the Manifest Sphere of Geburah. *Liber AL* tells us that "the Khabs is in the Khu, not the Khu in the Khabs." KHU is the Quantum particle of Will, and the dynamic energy of MARS=YOU resides herein, inside the Tower or House of God as it were, rather than the other way round with individuated pure Will existing inside the principle of Geburah's force. The inference is of course that the striking down of the tower is self-inflicted; the alchemist's own substance is the material being refined. It

is balanced by the more benign moral qualities of MENTU in the Manifested Chesed. The Key Grapheme is the letter-symbol S, the wave-form shape resumed again by the E. Qaballistic value which is 5.

17. KA understood as the spark or essence of a person's life is attributed to Aquarius and the Star. Aquarius the Water-Bearer is associated with Lucifer the Light-Bearer in the E. Qaballistic cosmology as follows. ONE LIGHT = 110 = LUCIFER; Lucifer is one light where ONE=A. A LIGHT = 65 = WATER; the nature of Water resonates with the nature of the one light which is carried by Lucifer. The one light is known as THE STAR=AQUARIUS the Water-bearer where BEARER=AQUARIUS, and is named MORNING STAR = 144 = CALLED AQUARIUS. In terms of the Zodiacal life-line this Sign carries the light from Capricorn to Pisces in readiness for birth at Aries. The letter-symbol L is the Key Grapheme, and it is naturally repeated in Manifest Malkuth.

18. RA-HOOR-KHUT has the same E. Qaballistic value as Pisces. PISCES=97=NOTHING is the Container of Heaven. Therefore it is placed at the top of the Complete Tree, as Unmanifested Kether, with the First Key of II:76, the symbol-number 4. In the Tarot Pisces is the Zodiac Sign attributed to the Moon: in the model of the Complete Tree we have already noted that the Perfected Lunar Sphere of Unmanifest Yesod is also given the repeated symbol-number 4, under the Name of HOOR PAAR KRAAT=THE LIGHT.

19. NU the wave-form of Light is attributed to the Sun and Tiphareth in Manifestation; Hadit is hidden in the 93 section of the Tree. In accordance with mystical tradition, there is a relationship between Tiphareth the Sephirah of

the Son and Kether, the Father, for in this model the Key Grapheme of the Manifest Tiphareth is the letter-symbol T, where the E.Q. value 24 is the Key symbol-number ascribed to Manifest Kether.

20. NUIT has the same E. Qaballistic value as FIRE, 78. Attributed to Unmanifest Chokmah and the 2nd Key of II:76 which is the symbol-number 6=LAW, this correspondence is balanced across the Cosmic Tree by the Element of Water, and resumed in the transforming force of Chokmah in Manifestation.

21. RA HOOR KHU has the same E. Qaballistic value as SATURN, 73, and is accordingly ascribed to Binah in Manifestation and the 21st Key Grapheme, the letter-symbol R. This letter is also that of the 15th Grapheme of II:76 and appears in the 93 section where it is ascribed to Virgo and the Name ISA, reflecting the Sorrows of Isis. 73=POWER, an appropriate balance against the Manifest Chokmah.

We have now accounted for 22 of our 28 Names. The three outer planets Uranus, Neptune, and Pluto, correspond to Manifest Kether, Perfect Malkuth/Da'ath, and Manifest Chokmah as follows.

Uranus is ascribed to Manifest Kether, along with HAD=11 (the first word of *Liber AL*) whose value recalls the symmetry of the Creation. The E. Qaballistic value of URANUS is the same as EARTH, 66, (6x11) in accordance with experiences of the Middle Pillar Meditation wherein Kether reflexes to Malkuth. The astrological nature of the planet tends towards the quick violence of the lightning bolt and thus accords with the dynamism of the Primum Mobile. It is thus revealed as a transition between the final X of the 93 section and the transformational force of the second Sephirah. HAD=11which is half the value of X=22, and the two 1's recall the "half of the word" (of Heru Ra Ha) which is ascribed to Chokmah in Manifestation as we will presently show. The Key Grapheme of Kether in Manifestation is the symbol-number 24, the value of GOD.

HERU-PA-KRAATH=136 and exists somewhere beyond Manifestation, an understanding supported by 136=BETWEEN which is the only other word in AL of this value. 136 = A BRILLIANCE, THE SHRINE, THIS WORSHIP, also suggesting a mystical quality: we therefore correlate this Name to the symbol of Neptune and the Cosmic or Unmanifest Malkuth which is placed in Da'ath. The watery nature of the planetary deity accords with the characteristic of our own ocean-rich world; astrologically speaking, Neptune is also concerned with gases and ethereal forms, and this is shown by the repetition of the Key Grapheme of AL II:76 belonging to Unmanifest Malkuth, the letter-symbol A, in the spheres ascribed to ARIES=EARTH and to the Moon.

HERU RA HA =76=PLUTO. *Liber AL* refers to the half of this entity's word "...called Hoor-pa-kraat and Ra Hoor Khut..." thereby suggesting correspondence with GEMINI=117=THE LIGHT and HOOR-PAAR-KRAAT, and with PISCES=97=NOTHING, RA HOOR KHUT, and the reverse value or Reward of HEAVEN=79. These are correspondences which illuminate Chokmah in Manifestation, by demonstrating that the half of the word described in AL I:47, "they [the Jews] have the half" is the Tree of Manifestation – where the other half is, of course, the Perfected Unmanifest Cosmic Tree with Hoor Paar Kraat/Gemini in Yesod and Ra Hoor Khut/Pisces in Kether. Pluto is the planet of Transformation, and the God of the Underworld. The Key Grapheme is the number-symbol 89 where 8 is Infinite and 9 is Illusion.

To the Sphere of Malkuth in Manifestation we assign the element of Earth and the Name TUM, and the encircled Equal-armed Cross. TUM has the same E. Qaballistic value as DOOR which is how we enter or depart from the holy place; as a God he is thought to be one of the first creations of the ancient pantheons. The Key Grapheme is the letter-symbol L, which is also the letter of the Eleventh Key which begins the 93 section. To that Key is ascribed the Name KA and the Zodiac Sign of Aquarius, both associated with the containing of Water or Spiritual Light; and when we look for some resonance or echo through the repetition of the Key letter, we find that planet Earth is itself also a Water-Bearer. We may take this correspondence further, refining it along the way to the Sphere of Unmanifested Hod, where the symbol-number 2 is the Key Grapheme and is the value of the letter L.

We complete our tally with the 6th letter-symbol of AL II:76, B=20 (the root number of MANIFESTATION=200), and the Name JESUS which we put in the Heavenly Tiphareth as an infinite Element of pure Spirit, symbolised by a five-pointed star; and finally with the Name KHU which we assign to the eighteenth letter-symbol, the X in the 93 section. It is conceptualised as a quantum of consciousness, the soul-singularity characterised by the element of the WILL=30=KHU; and symbolised with the encircled 'X'. 30 is also the value of HOOR which seems to be a generic name for all the Horus-type deities and suggests an inherent duality of identity. It is worth noting that the phrase "I AM LIFE" adds to 113 which is the value of SPIRIT and QUANTUM, and the number of the Perfect

Tiphareth as it manifests in Time; and that the words "I AM" (whose total value is 45=HORUS) counted well give the number 68=LIFE. The E. Qaballistic revelation of JESUS=68=LIFE has been explained at length in my first book, *The Magickal Language of the Book of the Law – an English Qaballa Primer*, published in 2016 by Hadean Press.

To sum up the foregoing as regards the placement of these twenty-eight Named principle symbols and their particular characteristics upon the pattern of the Complete Tree, we retain the traditional planetary attributions of the Sephiroth at the level of Manifestation, adding the Element of Earth at Malkuth, and Pluto and Uranus to Chokmah and Kether as previously mentioned. The Top Tree then has Pisces in Kether, the Element of Fire in Chokmah, and the Element of Water in Binah. Capricorn resides in Chesed and Aries is assigned to the Heavenly Geburah. At the centre of Heaven is the Element of Spirit. Taurus and the Element of Air correspond with the Cosmic Netzach and Hod respectively; to Yesod is ascribed Gemini, and Neptune as we have said is attributed to the Perfect Malkuth/Da'ath.

The 93 section is delineated as follows: Libra is at the central 'O' which is the point of balance of the model. On the left is Scorpio and on the right is Virgo, occupying the positions of the 'M' and the 'R'. Leo and Cancer are at the 'G' and '3' positions, and at the far left is Aquarius the Light-Bearer while Sagittarius is at the far right, corresponding with the 'L' and the 'Y'. Finally, the place of the letter 'X' in the 93 section is assigned to the Quantum Element of Will. Note that the seven above-mentioned Zodiac Signs Aquarius, Leo, Scorpio, Libra, Virgo, Cancer, and Sagittarius, are ruled by the traditional seven planets including the luminaries; appearing on the Unmanifest Tree are the remaining five Zodiac Signs Aries, Taurus, Gemini, Capricorn, and Pisces, traditionally ruled by Mars, Venus, Mercury, Saturn, and Jupiter.

ADDITIONAL REMARKS

The seven Spheres above the X describe a fully operational alchemical laboratory. In the centre stands the fateful Balance, and the Scales that will tip at a feather's weight, flanked by the two Zodiac Signs whose shapes recall the mysteries of the letter M; Virgo the Virgin and Scorpio the Bringer of Death, where VIRGIN=SCORPIO. The two luminaries of Sun and Moon are on either side of them; Hrumachis the child in the Sign of Silence supports SILENT=SCORPIO, and the gravid Khephra protective and concerned with more formative secrets (MOTHER=SCORPIO) is also standing guard as it were; and at the far ends we have the means by which the Light or Spiritual Essence is mobilised by the HEREAFTER=SAGITTARIUS and by THE STAR=AQUARIUS. These are the Seven Powers between unmanifest existence beyond Space-Time (sometimes called Heaven) and manifest spatial existence in Time (called the Universe). When the Sphere of Malkuth is perfected in manifestation it is immediately transmuted beyond spatial existence through Yesod to the perfection of Da'ath, by way of Unmanifest Geburah and the first Zodiac Sign, Aries, emblematic of birth; the same thing happens in reverse of course.

The seven Key Graphemes L, G, M, O, R, 3, and Y, have the combined value 71 = VENUS. This Goddess and this archetypal force of Nature is on the other side of the whirling X above Manifest Kether.

Ascribed to the 93 section are seven Zodiacal Principles, and the Principle of Will. The seven planets of antiquity rule the seven Zodiac signs: their qualities are therefore the basis of the Individuality. Aquarius(Saturn)=L; Leo(Sun)=G; Scorpio(Mars)=M; Libra(Venus)=O; Virgo(Mercury)=R; Cancer(Moon)=3; Sagittarius(Jupiter)=Y. These seven Zodiacal Principles inform the planetary Principles of the Personality which function along similar lines to the traditional Hebrew pattern, Pluto(Chokmah) receiving his authority from Taurus (the Perfected Netzach) and Uranus(Kether) reflexing from the Earth Principle. (PLUTO=76=TAURUS, URANUS=66=EARTH).

The Principle of Libra is assigned to the central O of the 93 section. The ruler of this Zodiac sign is Venus, the Goddess of Love. Her number, 7, is the value of O. The value of the Glyphs L G M O R 3 Y is 71=VENUS, which accords with the tradition that Venus contains all the planets. Only Love could exist in the perfect balance (Libra) between Unmanifest and Manifest, perpetually dividing and uniting in the heart of TIME=93, and only the pure Principle of Will can order its direction.

Let us return for a moment to the whole symbol of the Two Trees and see if we can find human correspondences. We observe that there are three sections, and we assign the Bottom Tree to the Personality, the 93 section to the Individuality, and the Top Tree to the Spirit. Now in the physical realm we can see the ten Principles of Spirit existing in another dimension as it were above Da'ath in Manifestation, between the top of the spine and the cranium and masked by the face. The 8 Principles of the

Individuality correspond to the spine and torso, along with all the vital organs; and the ten Principles of the Personality in the legs and feet, which carry the rest of the magickian about the Earth. Note that the lower Tree has no Da'ath sephirah: this is accessed through the Mind-Mirror of Manifest Yesod with the expansion of Malkuth-manifested consciousness.

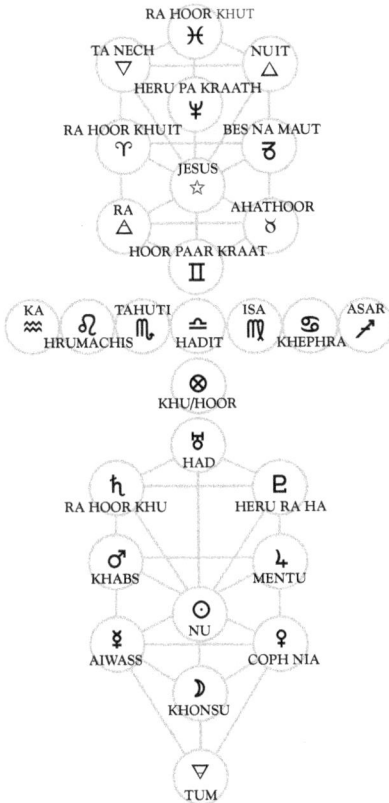

DIAGRAM 2: THE 28 NAMES AND SYMBOLS ON THE COMPLETE TREE OF LIFE

The following investigation was carried out with the purpose of discovering a structural framework for ritual in correlation with the (approximately) 28-day lunar cycle, in accordance with the second stage of our intended experiment. The correspondences we have proposed above were proved by this practical application.

In order to attribute the English Alphabet to the Complete Tree we began by simply placing the letters in their Qaballistic order with the Graphemes of II:76 so that Unmanifest Kether has "A", Unmanifest Chokmah has "L", Unmanifest Binah has "W", and so on down the Complete Tree to Manifest Hod, which has "P". This arrangement leaves Yesod and Malkuth in Manifestation with no English Qaballistic alphabetical letters, and so we take those two Spheres to represent the Inner and Outer existence of the operator. The system is approached or "switched on" from the last two Spheres, attributed to the Graphemes "A" and "L" by AL II:76. The preceding twenty-six Spheres from "4" to "V" are harmonised from the Perfect Tiphareth ("B") and manifested in Time through "X" at the end of the 93 section. These factors thus inform the necessary existence of Yesod and Malkuth in Manifestation.

The arrangement of the 28 Graphemes into four groups of seven followed, with three sets of seven English letters and one set of five. The first three groups of English letters may each be arranged so as to form a triangle whose sides have the same numeric totals, while the last group forms an equal-armed Cross with numeric equivalence

FINDING NEW SYMBOLS

across parallel diagonals. These groupings were used in constructing sigils intended to contact the hypothetical 28 Named magickal forces.

A division of the 28 Key Graphemes of AL II:76 with their assigned Names into four groups of seven provided another table:

4,6,3,8,A,B,K	2,4,A,L,G,M,O	R,3,Y,X,24,89	P,S,T,O,V,A,L
Ra Hoor Khut	Ra	Isa	Mentu
Nuit	Hoor Paar Kraat	Khephra	Khabs
Ta Nech	Heru Pa Kraath	Asar	Nu
Bes Na Maut	Ka	Khu/Hoor	Coph Nia
Ra Hoor Khuit	Hrumachis	Had	Aiwass
Jesus	Tahuti	Heru Ra Ha	Khonsu
Ahathoor	Hadit	Ra Hoor Khu	Tum

TABULATION OF II:76 IN FOUR COLUMNS WITH CORRESPONDING NAMES IN LIBER AL

We tested this arrangement with a series of rituals and found that each set of seven conceals a hierarchical group of spirits, having characteristics in common with the nature of their corresponding symbol. This brought our experiment to its fourth stage: to prove the existence of the 28 Spirits by repeated performance of the invocations, and investigation of their individual rank, characteristics, and abilities.

This fourfold arrangement is more fully tabulated below, between two columns of E.Q. values. The E. Qaballistic Alphabet is given at the far left-hand side, and in the far right-hand column is the total gematria of the line, comprising English letter value, Key Grapheme value, principle Symbol value, and Name value. The second column, headed "SPHERE", consists simply of the English names of the Sephiroth, and is intended to convey whatever the basic understanding is of these principles both as the set of ten manifested archetypal forces and the set of ten unmanifest perfections that inform them. The template of the Complete Tree is a useful tool for keeping track of all these different concepts. The third column, "Grapheme" gives the 28 Keys of Al II:76 which have delineated the divisions from the "old time" and united the "new symbols" of the E. Qaballistic system with universal occult heritage. The fourth column, "SYMBOL" reveals the nature of the forces which may be unlocked by using these Keys as navigational aids, and the fifth column "NAME" shows the particular Name from the text of *Liber AL* to be used when attempting to access a given force.

It should be understood that these Names are not specific identity tags of invisible anthropomorphic characters: they are phonetic symbols representing forces or principles of existence which may be understood and negotiated with through experience, knowledge, and understanding of their myths, their qaballistic symbolism, their associated ideas and stories, and the ways in which they interact with each other by reflexing or resonating similar or opposing concepts. They are flexible rather than

FINDING NEW SYMBOLS

fixed, inclined to blend and blur at the edges rather than existing separately as divided units; although they are only able to do what their nature suggests, somewhat as an actor in character is limited in improvisational work by the part he has assumed. Thus Venus and Mars for example are not inimical to each other, they are brother and sister after all, and there is much symbolism between them that shares bloodlust and passion. In E. Q. the Reward of VENUS=71 is 17=HAWK; there are bees among the emblems upon The Emperor Tarot card, assigned to Aries whose ruler is Mars; the Tarot card of Mars, The Tower, conceals one of the Mysteries of Isis, and TOWER=71=VENUS. But Venus is always the beautiful virgin and Mars the strong warrior, she can no more wield the Sword than he would know what to do with a Lamp. She would become Babalon, and he The Hermit – but that is another story.

LETTER	SPHERE	Grapheme	SYMBOL
A=1	PERFECT KETHER	4	PISCES
L=2	PERFECT CHOKMAH	6	FIRE
W=3	PERFECT BINAH	3	WATER
H=4	PERFECT CHESED	8	CAPRICORN
S=5	PERFECT GEBURAH	A	ARIES
D=6	PERFECT TIPHARETH	B	SPIRIT
O=7	PERFECT NETZACH	K	TAURUS
Z=8	PERFECT HOD	2	AIR
K=9	PERFECT YESOD	4	GEMINI
V=10	PERFECT MALKUTH (DA'ATH)	A	NEPTUNE

TABULATED CORRESPONDENCES OF E.Q., II:76, SYMBOLIC ELEMENT,

NAME	EQ SUM
RA HOOR KHUT	199
NUIT	164
TA-NECH	152
BES-NA-MAUT	261
RA HOOR KHUIT	192
JESUS	207
AHATHOOR	152
RA	59
HOOR PAAR KRAAT	247
HERU PA KRAATH	292

AND NAMES IN LIBER AL, ON THE TOP TREE

LETTER	SPHERE	Grapheme	SYMBOL
G=11		L	AQUARIUS
R=12		G	LEO
C=13		M	SCORPIO
N=14		O	LIBRA
Y=15		R	VIRGO
J=16		3	CANCER
U=17		Y	SAGITTARIUS
F=18		X	WILL

TABULATED CORRESPONDENCES OF E.Q., II:76, SYMBOLIC ELEMENT,

FINDING NEW SYMBOLS

NAME	EQ SUM
KA	118
HRUMACHIS	157
TAHUTI	220
HADIT	137
ISA	119
KHEPHRA	178
ASAR	197
KHU	100

AND NAMES IN LIBER AL, ON THE 93 SECTION.

LETTER	SPHERE	Grapheme	SYMBOL
Q=19	MANIFEST KETHER	24	URANUS
B=20	MANIFEST CHOKMAH	89	PLUTO
M=21	MANIFEST BINAH	R	SATURN
X=22	MANIFEST CHESED	P	JUPITER
I=23	MANIFEST GEBURAH	S	MARS
T=24	MANIFEST TIPHARETH	T	SUN
E=25	MANIFEST NETZACH	O	VENUS
P=26	MANIFEST HOD	V	MERCURY
	MANIFEST YESOD	A	MOON
	MANIFEST MALKUTH	L	EARTH

TABULATED CORRESPONDENCES OF E.Q., II:76, SYMBOLIC ELEMENT,

NAME	EQ SUM
HAD	120
HERU RA HA	261
RA HOOR KHU	179
MENTU	292
KHABS	106
NU	115
COPH NIA	191
AIWASS	189
KHONSU	106
TUM	130

AND NAMES IN LIBER AL, ON THE BOTTOM TREE.

The gematria in the far-right hand column serves to prove the attributions. Thus for example the total assigned to Manifest Yesod is the value of BECAUSE and STARLIGHT and I LOVE YOU, while that of Unmanifest Yesod is the value of TAKE YOUR FILL OF LOVE, SMELLING PERFUME, SACRED HEART AND TONGUE, and ALL PLEASURE AND PURPLE. The total value ascribed to the Perfect Tiphareth is 207; phrases of this value in *Liber AL* include THE FALL OF BECAUSE, IN THE CLEAR LIGHT, LORD INITIATING, and HELP ME O WARRIOR LORD. The central "O" has the total value of A SECRET DOOR (=137), and on either side are "M" whose total is 220 = DEATH IS THE CROWN OF ALL and "R" where the value is 119 = THE EARTH, and CREATION. Of course there are many more words and phrases in *Liber AL* that have these values; we have given enough to validate the demonstration.

THE MANSIONS OF THE MOON

Now to test this tabulated arrangement with a series of synchronised rituals, we will look at the correspondences to the Mansions of the Moon, which are of course 28 in number, a division of the Heavens reaching far back into antiquity (see tables on pages 44-49).

Note that the point of 0 Aries is ascribed to the Unmanifest Binah, the third Perfect Sephirah, rather than the first, the Perfection of Kether, which is symbolised by PISCES=RA HOOR KHUT=NOTHING. The nature of ARIES=EARTH=BABE is of something in imminent existence, which cannot be NOTHING. Moving the sequence of the Lunar Mansions down the table by a couple of notches as it were allows for the continuity of existence flowing from Manifest Malkuth back to Unmanifest Kether in an unbroken stream – it should be remembered that this is a cyclic progression and not linear and therefore is without beginning or end, and that the top-to-bottom diagrammatic arrangement is for convenience only.

(We must thank Jake Stratton-Kent for the Mansion Titles, and Vivian Robson for the information regarding the determinant stars.)

SYMBOL	KEY grapheme	MANSION
PISCES	4	4 Pisces
FIRE	6	17 Pisces
WATER	3	0 Aries
CAPRICORN	8	13 Aries
ARIES	A	26 Aries
SPIRIT	B	9 Taurus
TAURUS	K	21 Taurus
AIR	2	4 Gemini
GEMINI	4	17 Gemini
NEPTUNE	A	0 Cancer

Tabulated Correspondences of Symbolic Element, Grapheme,

FINDING NEW SYMBOLS

TITLE (longitude and English of determinant Star)
2nd Drawing. (5 36' The Lucky Star of Hidden or Hiding Things)
Pisces. (28 15' The Fore-spout of the Water-Bucket)
Horns of Aries. (8 2' The Second or Lower Spout)
Belly of Aries. (29 17' The Belly of the Fish)
Pleiades. (2 51' The Two Signs)
Eye or Head of Taurus. (27 54' The Belly)
Orion's Head. (28 52' The Many Little Ones) ARIES
Little Star of Great Light, 3 stars in Orion's shoulder. Contains Algol at 26 4'. (8 40' The Follower)
Arm of Gemini. (22 35' A White Spot)
Misty or Cloudy. (7 59' A Brand or Mark)

AND LUNAR MANSION, ON THE TOP TREE.

SYMBOL	KEY grapheme	MANSION
AQUARIUS	L	13 Cancer
LEO	G	26 Cancer
SCORPIO	M	9 Leo
LIBRA	O	21 Leo
VIRGO	R	4 Virgo
CANCER	3	17 Virgo
SAGITTARIUS	Y	0 Libra
WILL	X	13 Libra

TABULATED CORRESPONDENCES OF SYMBOLIC ELEMENT, GRAPHEME,

FINDING NEW SYMBOLS

TITLE (longitude and English of determinant Star)
Eye of the Lion. Contains Sirius at 13 57'. (19 8' The Forearm)
Neck or Forehead of the Lion. (6 7' [Leo] The Gap or Crib)
Mane. Contains the Aselli 8 35'. (16 46' The Glance of the Lion's Eye)
Tail. Contains Regulus 29 41'. (28 43' The Forehead)
Wings of Virgo or Dog Stars. (10 12' The Mane)
Spike of Virgo or Flying Spike. (20 30' The Weather-Changer)
Covered or Covered Flying. (26 2' [Virgo]The Barker)
Horns of Scorpio. Contains Spica 23 & Arcturus 24.(22 43' The Unarmed)

SYMBOL	KEY grapheme	MANSION
URANUS	24	26 Libra
PLUTO	89	9 Scorpio
SATURN	R	21 Scorpio
JUPITER	P	4 Sagittarius
MARS	S	17 Sagittarius
SUN	T	0 Capricorn
VENUS	O	13 Capricorn
MERCURY	V	26 Capricorn
MOON	A	9 Aquarius
EARTH	L	21 Aquarius

TABULATED CORRESPONDENCES OF SYMBOLIC ELEMENT, GRAPHEME,

FINDING NEW SYMBOLS

TITLE (longitude and English of determinant Star)
Crown of Scorpio. (2 40' [Scorpio] The Covering)
Heart of Scorpio. (13 58' The Claws)
Tail of Scorpio. Contains Serpentis 19. (2 4' [Sagittarius] The Crown of the Forehead)
A Beam. (8 39' The Heart)
A Desert. (23 28' The Sting)
Head of Capricorn – a Pastor. (12 31' The Ostriches)
Swallowing. Contains Deneb 19 & Vega 15. (15 8' The City or District)
Star of Fortune. (2 42' [Aquarius] The Lucky One)
A Butterfly or Spreading Forth. (11 53' The Good Fortune of the Swallower [i.e. the Receiver])
1st Drawing. (22 17' The Luckiest of the Lucky)

AND LUNAR MANSION, ON THE BOTTOM TREE

The correspondences across this Table join some interesting dots in a rather illuminating fashion. The Pastor in the sphere of Manifest Tiphareth, for example; Saturn at The Scorpion's Tail where the paralysing poison awaits; the Aselli in Scorpio; Jesus at the Eye of the Bull. We cannot analyse too closely though, since the passage of time has obscured much of the original tradition with attributions from different systems, as well as "moving" the positions of fixed stars by the Precession of the Equinoxes, and we have to look at the ideas which have survived these erosions in very soft focus to get any sense out of them. The good fortune of the swallower is perhaps more relevant to a pre-historic desert traveller than a 21st Century urban dweller, for the former will otherwise die, while the latter is more assured of accessing clean water; or this may be part of a charm, a blessing, or "grace" uttered before consumption of meat and drink. Other correspondences are more blatant – for example, in this schema the configuration of the Lion's Mane is doubly attributed to both Scorpio and Virgo, on either side of the central O of MOR in the 93 section, a startling confirmation of the proposed attributions.

We may conduct a more useful operation of analysis and synthesis by examining the attributions of single Graphemes from II:76 across all of these tabulations. We will begin with Tiphareth in Manifestation, whose character and symbolism is immediately familiar, and see if we can detect any parallels. Our third Table gives the following:

T=24 | MANIFEST TIPHARETH | T | SUN |
NU | =115

and the same line on Table No.4 reads:

SUN | T | 0 Capricorn | Head of Capricorn – a
Pastor (12 31' THE OSTRICHES)

Apart from the obvious ostrich-plumes on the crowns and headdresses of Egyptian deities associated with balance and justice and righteous rulership, the ostrich itself is traditionally associated with royalty. It is a difficult creature to hunt, capable of outpacing a camel, hiding itself by laying down where it makes a rounded silhouette easily mistaken for a terrain feature, and able to fight with strong kicking legs and hard pecking beak; prowess and honour are therefore due to the successful hunter. The ostrich will leave its eggs unattended for the shells are too hard for most predators: and containing plenty of richly flavoured meat, they are a gift fit for a king.

The meaning of the English word "Pastor" is derived from translations of Latin words such as the noun "pastor" meaning "shepherd" and the verb "pascere" meaning "to lead to pasture, to set to graze" and thus it broadly describes the ideal character and activity of a spiritual leader, who harmonises and sustains the congregation. In purely zoomorphic terms the head of the goat does the same thing for the body of the goat; there is also good eating in the head of a goat when the animal has been spit-roasted whole in the customary way.

So far we have assembled ideas of nourishing and sustaining in body and spirit, of excellence and majesty and of good order, which accord nicely with the traditional symbolism of Tiphareth. The association with Capricorn reminds us of Baphomet, whose head is that of an Ass;

and the astrological attribution of Capricorn is to the Tenth House which represents the ruling authority in the chart, the Judge in a court of Law, for instance; these correspondences also serve to fill in the picture as it were. Now we may trace a link to the old system through the Key English letter T to the Hebrew letter Tau, traditionally ascribed to Saturn, which rules Capricorn. We may observe that T=24 = GOD: and this is an odd juxtaposition, for GO-D is the GO – LAW(=D) or Law of Going (which as Crowley said is a prime function of the Magickian) as we would expect to find exemplified in a wandering animal such as a goat, while Saturn is a crystallising sort of a force which makes things slow down and stop. It is like the confining of energy by coiling the spring; but here we are concerned with the activity of the energy once it has reacted with the restriction of Binah, been shaped and refined by Chesed and Geburah, and achieved this dynamic harmony of Force and Form in the central sixth Sphere. The fact that this is the Twenty-Fourth Key means that in the order and value of the English Alphabet the corresponding letter is again T -- an emphasis which is not accidental.

The Scapegoat comes in here, the creature used by the community or tribe to embody all their acts requiring atonement and sent out into exile to get on with atoning on their behalf. Once more we have to thank the scholars who translated the Bible into English for the word which comes from roots meaning "the remover" or "the sender away" – of sin – although the practice in ancient times was not exclusive to the Hebrew tradition. It seems a rather unlikely working of sympathetic magic by 21st century Western Occult standards when the whole notion of "sin"

FINDING NEW SYMBOLS

is open to question, and animal sacrifice is frowned upon by society. And yet there may be virtue in the process when more specifically applied. Again, the general idea is of lawful judgement, order, harmony, and a sustainable structure, but now we are coming to the notion of the sacrifice which is necessary to maintain the idea. It is simply that in order to effect a change such as may be necessary for survival, energy must be used in transmutation from what was to what is desired to be. Precisely how the change comes about is a mystery, much as the Scapegoat's activities in exile remain unknowable.

This mystery is analogous to the question of where the Sun goes at night, and this is why the sacrificial deities are by tradition assigned to Tiphareth, the Sphere of the Sun. The symbolism is huge, and beyond our present remit, but not at all difficult to access from a variety of different sources and traditions. We must leave that to the reader, and move on to the Name from the Lexicon of *Liber AL* assigned to this Sphere. That Name is NU = 31 = SOUL and WORK and GOOD.

The shape of the letters "n" and "u" suggest the crest and trough of a wave, a shape echoed in the letter "S" which combines with the first two letters to make the word "Sun". AL tells us the Nu is the hiding of Hadit, the infinitely tiny particle that cannot be observed except by means of an almost infinitely tiny wave-form (light) which is ever-so-slightly bigger than the tiny particle. The tiny particle must be the smaller of the two phenomena, and its presence is thus effectively hidden by the wave-form of the light that returns the image to us. The physicists who experiment at these levels tell us that the phenomenon we call light is capable of behaving as a wave-form or as a particle, and it all gets a bit confusing; the point to remember is that Nu is the wave-form of light which hides the tiny perfection of Hadit, as the light of the Sun hides what the Sun actually is. For the present purpose we may conceive of the Sun as the entrance to Heaven, or the Gate of the Great God, or the Brilliance before the Face of The One, or the centre of an infinitely large sphere, or even as an open wormhole in space leading to some unimaginable dimension: it does not really matter. Nu is the means by which we are able to perceive such with our naked eyes, and also which hides the reality of its true nature from us. The correspondence with the word SOUL will reveal much to the reader who includes the notion of Soul in their personal cosmogony; the physics should enable the more sceptical mind to achieve a similar comprehension of these factors; GOOD is a pretty obvious correspondence for anyone, and WORK is a term of some significance to many occultists in the Western Traditions – including those who "don't do God" and/or have little sympathy for esoteric philosophy in science, but who may find the present treatise of interest.

The tabulated value of the E.Q. letter T (24) and the value of the Key Grapheme (T=24) together with the value of the Symbol (SUN=36) and the value of the Name (NU=31) all add up to 115 = PRIEST, and also MERCURY, MOON+URANUS/EARTH, and MARS+PLUTO. This is a rich vein of astro-magickal symbolism which we cannot explore extensively here; it will suffice to say the ideas are primarily of transforming, transmuting, and ritualising. Phrases from Liber AL which add to 115 include "LOVE OF ME...NOT FAITH...GOD TO LIVE...THE KINGS... AGELONG LOVE...SWEET WORDS...YOUR LIGHT...

WORK THE WORK...FOURFOLD WORD...I AM THE HAWK." The last is a sharp reminder of the requirement for resistance to onrushing energy for the production of a result.

These words may be allowed to flow through the mind like perfume during a meditation, or used aloud as part of an E. Qaballistic invocation. Here it is worth noting that these tend to be extempore, often employing repetition as with a mantra, the E. Qaballistic ritualist(s) having a sufficient enumerated vocabulary for the immediate application and/or recognition of appropriately significant words and phrases. A group working these kinds of ceremonies often spontaneously "discovers" (or is inspired towards) an appropriate chanting rhythm, over which the invocation becomes a melody. This sort of thinking allows for substitution of some words for others of the same value from the Lexicon of *Liber AL* but not written together in the manuscript: thus "NOT FAITH" becomes "I AM FAITH" since I AM = 45 = NOT. (This also is an important magickal formula which the reader may discern from examining the values and context of the phrase in *Liber AL* I:58).

To return to the number 115, as the combination of the Key, the Symbol, the Name, and the position in the sequence of the 28, (24 + 36 + 31 + 24 = 115), the figure should help with the synthesis of the preceding assortment of correspondences and allow us to construct a portrait as it were of Tiphareth in Manifestation in this era of our magickal/spiritual development. In this context VIRTUOUS=115 and UNIQUE=115 are apt, but PRIEST=115 is clearly the most relevant and significant correspondence. We see a Priest-King (or an overriding state of consciousness) who sustains his people (or the characteristics of the individual concerned) and leads them into a propitious future; whose rule is righteous and just; whose authority is supreme; who is qualified for sacrifice by his own experience; and whose glory is but the concealment of a Greater Glory. Now this interpretation is not so very different from certain other descriptions appropriate to the Sphere of the Sun, of which the reader may be aware; we leave the conclusions for the reader to devise.

The preceding paragraph was a rather bold assertion, at the end of a somewhat rambling argument. We will attempt therefore to justify it by applying the same analytical technique to the Nineteenth Key of II:76 and the Sphere of Kether in Manifestation. We should find the usual parallels quite easily, if we are on the right track. Our two tabulated lines of correspondences are, on Table No. 3:

Q=19 | MANIFEST KETHER | 24 | URANUS | HAD | =120

and from the fourth Table:

URANUS | 24 | 26 LIBRA | CROWN OF SCORPIO (2 40' [SCORPIO] THE COVERING

The word "Covering" conveys ideas of protection and concealment, and may refer to all sorts of materials and uses, from lids on jars to the roof of a dwelling, from the cloak to the death-shroud to the swaddling cloth; and in the context of the Crown of Scorpio the Emblem of Death we may perhaps think of the crown worn by the dead Osiris, or the executioner's hood, or the black cap worn by the Judge when passing the death sentence. The Stellar correspondence of Libra supports the association with Judgement.

The nineteenth letter in the order and value of the English Qaballistic Alphabet is "Q". This letter has the same pronunciation as the English word "queue" which comes from Old French words meaning "tail". One of the meanings of "queue" is a plait of hair worn at the back of the head; it also means a line of people (or data, in computing terminology) waiting for attention; the emphasis is on the back of the head, in accordance with the equivalent Hebrew letter "Qoph".

Uranus, the Symbol of this Key, is astrologically associated with the rapid action of electrical force and inventive inspiration; it has the same value as EARTH (66) which is fitting for the consort of the Earth-Mother Gaia. The life of the planet's discoverer, William Hersechel, appropriately spanned the birth and implementation of the Industrial Revolution in the 18th century's explosion of research and development in chemistry, physics, and engineering; in the same year was born M. Guillotine. We mention the latter because his invention ties in with our previous comments about the letter Q, the back of the head being the executioner's view, and because the force employed in the mechanism of the "little door" is also the energy behind the axe and the noose, generated over a given distance by the mass or weight of the falling object. This is, of course, gravity, an inexorable but necessary law which binds us all to the Earth.

Swift decapitation seems to be the order of the day, then. We may bring in all the ideas of the Headless One, and the Sacred Head; we may also be reminded of the blinding flash of white brilliance above the head that occurs with "high" mystic visions and near-death experiences; we may even note the unfortunate evidence of functioning consciousness remaining in the separated head for some seconds after execution. Perhaps in ancient times a great mystic came back from some very exalted state and reported his experience as "like having my head taken off by a flash of lightning". At any rate, there is a discernible link with the Name attributed to this Key, HAD. This is the first word of the *Book of the Law*, the full sentence being "Had! the manifestation of Nuit," which is equivalent to the Biblical "Let there be light!" Its value is 11, which as we know is the numeric clue to the cipher of the English Alphabet. It is a magickal formula of creative Change described in the words from AL 1:27-8, "...let...men speak not of Thee as One but as None...None, breathed the light...and Two".

Here, then, we are at the knife-edged watershed – just on this side of the blade – between being and not-being. Consciousness comes (or goes) in an instant, with the speed of a lightning bolt. Using the total E.Q. value of Key, Symbol, Name, and position (24 + 66 + 11 + 19 = 120) we find 120 = ESPECIAL...OVERCOME...THE FLAME... KNOWLEGE GO...OF THE STAR...OF THE CROSS...A CARESS OF HELL...WORD NOT KNOWN... EXALT ME...GOD AND BEAST...THE STAIN. These correspondences suggest a mystery of perilous dynamism. There is no morality here, only necessity. The initial separation of the individual consciousness of a human mind from the One Mind which is the unity of all consciousness has to occur for life to continue, and it has to be a fast, clean cut.

120 is also the value of Ra Hoor Khuit, a god "of vengeance," according to *Liber AL* III:3, and it is easy to see how the Sephirah of the Father became associated with revenge and punishment, but in our interpretation these are self-serving anthropomorphisms. We see only formulae and operations which are necessary for the continuity of existence, mysteries which are well within the knowledge and jurisdiction of the character depicted in our analysis of Tiphareth.

Now we will investigate the correspondences of Malkuth in Manifestation, where we should find some reflex from our Kether description, and thereby add to the proving of our proposed correspondences.

– – – | MANIFEST MALKUTH | L | EARTH |
TUM | =150

and

EARTH | L | 21 AQUARIUS | 1ˢᵗ DRAWING
(22 17' THE LUCKIEST OF THE LUCKY)

The "First Drawing" is most likely the first bucketful raised up from the bottom of the well. In a desert environment if there is water it would be fortunate, and if clean and drinkable then the Drawer could certainly be called "Luckiest of the Lucky". Another definition might be the preliminary sketch by an artist, which is the seed of the final work, and is also in a manner of speaking the refinement of the final work, for it should contain sufficient information to guide the artist to the completion of the piece; the phrase could also mean the first condensation in a process of distillation.

The constellation of Aquarius is always depicted as a water-bearer in the act of pouring; it is said to be the immortalisation of Ganymede, the beautiful youth who became the Cup-Bearer of the Gods. Here the interesting characteristic is the renowned beauty of this demi-god, supported by the peacock's feather symbol of this particular Zodiac sign. In E. Qaballistic terms he is analogous to Lucifer the Light Bearer, as we have said, WATER=A LIGHT, AQUARIUS=BEARER.

We can easily synthesise all of the foregoing remarks into an idea of the spark of life with a particular characteristic of good fortune, and an affinity with Venus the Goddess of Beauty and Nature.

The Key Grapheme is the letter L, with the E. Qaballistic value 2, indicating that our proposed spark is in a condition of duality. It is the duality inherent in our lives in manifestation, it is what we see at the other end of the telescope through which we earlier looked at Kether and what lies just this side of unmanifestation. We will leave the correspondences of the word "TWO" for the reader's contemplation, and move on to the Name, TUM.

In Ancient Egypt the God Atum or Atem (Tum) was the God who lifted the dead pharaoh to the heavens, finalising his earthly life and beginning his ascent to perfection; he was the first creator-god, producing the next generation from his own bodily fluids. His children were therefore the bearers of his water, and if we surmise that some substance was moulded into their forms with the aid of moisture, we can imagine the making of a doll and most importantly the making of the space for the life to dwell within. Then we might call this the "secret door, into the House of Ra and Tum" mentioned in AL III:38. Alternatively, we may prefer to look at some correspondences of the Name TUM=62 as follows: "SACRED...POUR...FALLEN... ANIMAL...LOCKED...KINGS...BOWELS...A COPY...A SHAPE...AN EGG...THY WAY". Here we can trace the signature of creation and the manifestation into form of unmanifest energy.

Finally, the sum total of 130 = BETTER, EQUATION (a puzzle of balance), MULTIPLY (as life is designed to do, 93 makes the DIVIDE(=93) and the ENDING(=93) that stops things getting out of hand), LITTLE WORLD, MY SISTER, and THE DOUBLE. All of these expressions support our idea of a spark or star, refined and fortunate, self-aware insofar as to apprehend its independence from its source, designed to illuminate and carry a life manifested in Time.

To complete our thesis of correlation between the Lunar Mansions and II:76 on the old Middle Pillar of the Kabbalists, we must evaluate the Sphere of Yesod using the same methods as before. The third Table gives:

– – – | MANIFEST YESOD | A | MOON | KHONSU | =106

and the same line on the fourth Table reads:

MOON | A | 9 AQUARIUS | A BUTTERFLY, OR SPREADING FORTH

The name of this Mansion's determining Star suggests an unfurling that might not stop, a fanning-out as of water spilling or running in flash flood over dry ground. The association with the Moon may suggest the way in which perfume spreads on the air, or the rhythm of the butterfly's wings; the appearance of the creature from its armoured chrysalis (which, being a life-bearer, we may assign to Aquarius) is an extraordinary event to witness, revealing the beauty of a new-born goddess. But it is a fragile, faery thing, easily broken.

We introduced the metaphor of the knife earlier, and now we are practically upon the knife-edge: it is a Woman's Knife, since the Key Letter is A=1 and ONE=WOMAN; and we may assume that it is consecrated in the Name of the moon-god KHONSU whose value is 56 =ISIS, and FEAR. Extreme care seems advisable, and indeed we should be gentle with our imagining minds or we may find Fear spreading like water and forcing a metamorphosis which we had only glimpsed and run away from. WISE=56=FACT, WINGS – these are what we may hope to gain here, what we might feel either around us or as part of our being. This is rather what one's first experiences with magical energies, such as are met with on the Astral plane, tend to be like, until we find our feet as it were and figure out the rules.

106=STARLIGHT, BECAUSE (the answer to Why, who is damned in AL, the argument is endless and only stopped by cessation (death) of one side due to conquest by the other, though this can be achieved both amicably and fast by magickal means) and MOHAMMED who surely understood this most subtle law.

The curious thing is that the preceding layout of Lunar Mansion correspondences we have proposed through our English Qaballistic studies seem to fit quite well with our experiences of the old Middle Pillar and the Hebrew Tree of Life. Of course, these descriptions have been to some extent subjective, but there is an undeniable consistency of the linking between the old traditions of Kabbalah and magical astronomy and the new symbols we have found, which may be deemed to prove the correctness of our attributions. We have the separation, lightning-fast, from beyond and into manifestation, reflected into a form capable of bearing the life-spark, equipped with a subtle consciousness, and able to comprehend the place from whence it came and must return, through and by the necessity of sacrifice. Now the only force which could account for all of that is LOVE, and therein is no morality, no grace and no guilt, simply that which is necessary for the Performance of the One Great Miracle.

Amen.

INTERMEDIATE CONCLUSIONS AND SUBSEQUENT EVENTS

The results experienced in ritual, meditation, and dreams confirmed our analyses. We had drawn tables and pushed the numbers as far as we could, and we could not find fault. That was pleasing to begin with but as the work went along it became a bit scary, as we felt more and more that we were being led by an unseen hand. We had proved our proposition and used the magical techniques of the grimoire traditions to contact spirits associated with *Liber AL*. Testing our correspondences against the Lunar Mansions should have been unsuccessful, but it wasn't, and we backed off.

We had formulated a Grimoire of English Qaballistic Magic, and found that it worked, in its own terms, and in our own experience. This did not mean that it would be of any use to anyone else, which from the beginning of English Qaballa was one of our benchmarks and final proofs. The next step would be to look for parallel characteristics in the goetic spirit catalogues, one or two of which we had noticed. The only question was whether we should engage with that adventure. A conjunction of the Sun and Venus close to the Spring Equinox was in the offing, and we took the opportunity to invoke the Lord and Lady of the Stars at this auspicious time and humbly ask for permission to continue, and for guidance.

A few days later, after a dream of particular joy which on waking left only a feeling of something wonderful and imminent, we were considering making illustrations of the spirits we had contacted, when suddenly another voice was heard, and the following dialogue took place.

"Do a Tarot."

"What?"

"Design a Tarot."

"An E.Q. Tarot? You must be kidding."

Silence, deep and velvety and amused.

"I'd never finish it!"

Silence. And as the moment passes the universe moves, and we all know it's too late, and that nothing will ever be the same again. We make one last futile protest against the irreversible.

"The world is awash with Tarot decks! Everyone and his acolyte has done a Tarot!"

"All the more reason for you to do one." Fast as a ricochet.

"But...but..."

There was nowhere to go.

"I'll need help. Lots of help. They're not my letters, I didn't make them. And they're not my symbols neither, and the numbers are nothing to do with me. I don't know how they all fit together. I'm not old enough, I'm not wise enough, I haven't the skill, I haven't the patience – seventy-eight cards? I'll never do it..."

Whatever we had said, our solution to the problem of positioning 26 letters in 28 places was unsatisfactory and we knew it. Even though we had derived a structural framework for timed Lunar rituals that demonstrably worked in its own terms, it was a system which focussed not on the symbolism of the letters themselves but on the patterns they make upon the Complete Tree. In the course of designing an E.Q. Tarot we would have to make a proper job of attributing the individual letters, including finding the answers for the two extra places.

We did not expect to succeed in this endeavour. We had never intended to make a Tarot. We certainly had not anticipated this development when we started. It is a logical expansion of the English Qaballistic system, and an equally logical evolution of the traditional Western Occult presentations of the Tarot symbolism. We were inspired, dragged, pushed, and instructed to do this Work. We demanded only a consistency of design throughout, and can take credit for nothing more than correct strokes of brush and pen.

PART TWO
THE E.Q. TAROT

THE FIRST TASK was to discover the attributions of the 26 letters to the 12 Signs of the Zodiac, the 4 Elements, and the 10 planets. In the course of this exploration it became clear that the Major Arcana of the new Tarot would be, apart from their divinatory use, mnemonic picture-symbols, which perhaps was the original function of the Tarot. The images will be discussed later on.

THE SYMBOLS AND THE LETTERS

The first three letters, A, L, W, have the total value of 6, and spell the word LAW=6, indicating the Harmony of Law associated with the 6th Sephirah, Tiphareth. The three Zodiac Signs assigned to these letters are SCORPIO, SAGITTARIUS, CAPRICORN, whose combined value is 360, the number of degrees in a circle. Once we have drawn the circle we can easily make the 6-pointed Star or Hexagram; these three Signs taken together thus embody the Law (whatever we understand that to be!) They are also three-quarters of the House known as 418, the number arrived at with the addition of 58=LIBRA and HOUSE: we will return to this Sign later on.

1=A. Here, the number ONE=46=WOMAN. At a very basic level, the human female can be defined as either Virgin or Mother, insofar as the creature has either given birth to a human child, or has not. Now by E.Q. both VIRGIN and MOTHER have the value 93, which is the value of SCORPIO. Woman is therefore intimately associated with the Sign of Scorpio. "Yet therefore is the knowledge of

ME=46=WOMAN the knowledge of Death." (AL II:6) Just as Woman brings forth Life, so does Woman attend to the ceremonies of Death. The haemorraging of blood is usually a sure indication of imminent mortality, and yet Woman does this every month and it is an indication of her ability to conceive a new life. Death itself may be an ENDING=93; it is also a moment in which to BEGIN=93. The shape of the letter "A" may suggest the completed Pyramid, or the infinitely tiny point coming into manifestation, etc.

2=L. This is the Duality of Creation wherein the division for love's sake transforms the UNITY=93 of One into "None, and Two." (AL I:28) The right-angle shape of the letter "L" may suggest two dimensions or planes of existence, or the first stages of construction design, or other combinations of two principles as implied in the figure of the Centaur. His Weapon is the aimed arrow; in the 418 cycle the Sagittarius phase is described as an arrow in flight, being the period immediately after death when the individual's life essences depart from the body and begin the journey beyond. SAGITTARIUS=146=HEREAFTER. The energy of this beginning is that which the artist employs in making the first marks upon the chosen surface, without knowing much about what will happen next.

3=W. In Kabbalistic terms we may say that this is the Binah (Saturnine) stage, the formation of the trinity which if left its own devices would become binding and permanently fixed. In the 418 cycle this is Capricorn, the final stage, exemplified by the nativity myths of the Winter Solstice wherein the Divine Light begins to dawn once more. THREE=PEACE by E.Q., which is the least we may expect and hope for after death.

The next four English letters follow the traditional planetary order of the Kabbalistic Tree of Life.

4=H. JUPITER=PERFECT by E.Q., a characteristic of the Chance decreed by Providence that keeps the manifest Universe running as it should, always just a step away from the Perfection that would annihilate all. JUPITER=TERRIBLE as well. Jupiter offers all kinds of wealth and expansion but there are always risks to be taken in the progress and evolution of Life. The symmetrical shape of the letter suggests stability and balance in design; it is the first letter of *Liber AL*, and 4 is the first number of AL II:76.

5=S, where the shapes of both number and letter describe the activity of the wave form or unit of energy. Mars is raw energy in all applications; in E.Q. the force is also that of the five-pointed star, the Pentagram, symbol of purification and exorcism.

6=D. The harmony inherent in the number 6 is always associated with the Sun. To the E. Qaballist the number is symbolic of the Law.

7=O. The untouchable pure beauty of the Goddess Venus (whose number is the lucky 7) is emphasised by the circular letter; the shape also means Zero or Nothing, a condition of purity.

8=Z. 8 is a symbol of Infinity in E.Q. as well as in mathematics; on the traditional Tarot card attributed to Mercury it is sometimes placed above the figure's head. The shape of the letter "Z" suggests the lightning stroke and thus the speed of thought, the swiftness of the intellect.

9=K. The number 9 is most often associated with the Yesodic Sephirah of Illusion, to which the Moon is traditionally assigned. In this context however, the symbolism is being considered primarily from a magickal-astrological standpoint, which in turn reveals Yesod as a veil in consciousness, at the edge of the waking mind, and thus disassociates its number from the astrologer's fastest luminary. Now we can take the whole Solar System as representing consciousness and, finding Pluto at the furthest distance from the centre, we may try the number 9 as a symbolic representation of the God of the Underworld, standing at the border of the mind. Pluto's influence is of Transformation and often manifests violently; in this respect there is a similarity with Mars, and we find that FIVE and NINE have the same E.Q. value which supports our attribution of the number 9 to the planetary Chakra of Pluto. The shape of the letter suggests a T-Cross leaning against a vertical straight line; expressing a particular condition of alteration or state of things in transition.

10=V. URANUS=66=EARTH to which the number 10 is traditionally assigned. The downward pointing letter may suggest a focus of intent, or pressure; or the invoking gesture of raising the arms, etc.

11=G, attributed to Neptune. It is a mysterious letter and a no less mysterious number which is the Key to the E. Qaballistic order and value of the English Alphabet, amongst other characteristics of this double numeral symbol. Da'ath is sometimes called "the eleventh Sephirah" and does not exist in the same plane as the other Sephiroth. It is worth noting that the eccentricity in Neptune's orbit sometimes takes it outside that of Pluto.

12=R is attributed to Saturn which in the 22-letter Tarot is a symbol of the Universe or the World. In this context, the furthest boundary of what man has knowledge of is the circle of the Zodiac whose twelve divisions are symbolised in E.Q. by the letter R=12. Note that the shape of the number 12 is similar to the shape of the letter R.

13=C is obviously attributable to the Moon for the crescent shape of the letter and the 13 lunar months which most nearly approximate the passage of one year. This is the halfway point of the 26 and the last of the planetary cards.

The following nine letters belong to the Zodiac.

14=N. The sequence continues with Pisces which is something of a reflection of the first letter due to the associations of the Fish and the letter "ﬡ" (1) with Death. PISCES=NOTHING=97 and its Reward is 79=HEAVEN; it is symbolic of the Perfect Tree in the model indicated by AL II:76. It is representative of the pre-birth stage of Human Life.

15=Y added to the value of AQUARIUS=95 gives the E.Q. value of LUCIFER=110. The Sign of Aquarius carries the Light from Capricorn through to Pisces from whence it is ready to be born in Aries. AQUARIUS=THE STAR which is the Light carried by Lucifer. It is a Sign of transition as may be inferred from the shape of the letter where we see one line being divided, or two lines being joined to make one, or three lines coming to a focal point; also from the sound of the letter "why" which is a question of great significance.

16=J and the number is a symbol of WAR to the E. Qaballist, the word being the only example in the Lexicon of *Liber AL* having that value. The attribution to the martial Zodiac Sign of Aries (Horus) is obvious; the shape of the letter and the harmonious 6 suggest a more intricate mystery of balancing.

17=U. Here the cup-shape of the letter indicates a containing, holding, possessing quality which aligns with the astrological attribution of Taurus to property, and rulership of the Sign by Venus. VENUS=71 and 17=HAWK; it is the hierophantic circling of birds of prey that shows the way to fresh meat.

18=F, and 18=GO, and G:O = 11:7, and 117=GEMINI. The word EIGHTEEN=151 is the highest numerical word in the Lexicon of Liber AL. With the same value as LIBRA+SCORPIO the number is symbolic of forces outside manifestation; and the formula by which they come into being is revealed through GEMINI=THE LIGHT, associated in E.Q. with the principle of Kether in Manifestation.

19=Q. The shape of the letter suggests the fertilised ovum appropriate to the Sign of the Mother and the Home, Cancer. In English usage the letter "Q" always appears with the letter "U" which supports our attributions, the Home being a primary possession and thus always linked with Taurus to which "U" is assigned.

20=B is considered by E. Qaballists to be the root number of MANIFESTATION=200 where TWO has the same value as LEO. The untarnished innocent passion of Leo, the House and Sign of the Child, is the dynamic power symbolised here; it is a Goddess rather than a God whom we approach, for the Zero or Nought is negative, and TWO=SHE.

21=M is another number-letter symbol steeped in occult tradition as the initial of the Magdalene, and the sum of 3x7 (which in E.Q. is equivalent to three forms of nothing). The attribution to the Sign of the Virgin is obvious.

22=X, an important symbol in the English Qaballa signifying the Ordeal X mentioned in AL III:22, "...and for the winners of the Ordeal X." Put simply, this is an ordeal of crossing from one condition to another; but it happens over and over again. (DAY=22). ORDEALS=58=LIBRA. The E. Qaballistic magickian experiences the Ordeal X repeatedly in all manner of different episodes and timeframes; it is also a terrifying Initiation in which the Candidate is led through the House of 418 from Libra the Sign of Justice to Capricorn (who is also the Judge and has the highest authority in astrological terms) where all conflict and duality is redeemed.

The last four English letters are attributed to the Elements.

23=I means the Individuality, the Identity, the self-aware consciousness, whose source and energy is delineated in the Element of Fire.

24=T has the same value as GOD in E.Q. The shape of the letter resembles a cross and so is appropriate to the sanctity and to the sacrifice of the attributed Element of Earth.

25=E has the same value as HAND, with which we both give and receive; it relaxes into a cupped shape, as if designed to default into a vessel for the Element of Water.

26=P. Pronunciation of this letter ejects a puff or tiny blast of air from the lips, making it the most effective for extinguishing a candle flame. The letter shape is most alike to one of the earliest hieroglyphs in the Egyptian script, which may represent a flag, or an axe, or a face in profile, or a mask; the other letter of similar shape, "F", symbolises what we may call "first principles of force". In the text of *Liber AL* there is no mention of the Element of Air; the word has the same value as SUN and MAN and is significant by its absence.

These attributions are tabulated below.

EQ	ATTRIBUTION	TAROT TITLE
1=A	SCORPIO	DEATH
2=L	SAGITTARIUS	ART
3=W	CAPRICORN	THE DEVIL
4=H	JUPITER	THE WHEEL OF FORTUNE
5=S	MARS	THE TOWER
6=D	SUN	THE SUN
7=O	VENUS	THE EMPRESS
8=Z	MERCURY	THE JUGGLER
9=K	PLUTO	THE THRESHOLD
10=V	URANUS	THE MAGICIAN
11=G	NEPTUNE	THE MYSTIC
12=R	SATURN	THE WORLD
13=C	MOON	THE PRIESTESS
14=N	PISCES	THE MOON
15=Y	AQUARIUS	THE STAR
16=J	ARIES	THE EMPEROR
17=U	TAURUS	THE HIEROPHANT

18=F	GEMINI	THE LOVERS
19=Q	CANCER	THE CHARIOT
20=B	LEO	STRENGTH
21=M	VIRGO	THE HERMIT
22=X	LIBRA	JUSTICE
23=I	FIRE	THE AEON
24=T	EARTH	THE HANGED MAN
25=E	WATER	THE CONCUBINE
16=P	AIR	THE FOOL

TABULATED CORRESPONDENCES OF E.Q. ALPHABET, SYMBOLIC
ELEMENTS, AND E.Q. TAROT TITLES

ON THE DESIGN OF THE 26 IMAGES

We started with the standard imagery and titles of the
22-card system, exploring the attributions to understand the
links between those suggested by the given title and those
suggested by the astrological or elemental characteristics
and qualities. Alterations were made where common sense
indicated, to accommodate the extra four letter-symbols.
Once we had arrived at a figurative portrayal drawn from
these sources, we looked at the E. Qaballistic attributions
to complete the design of each Trump.

The 26 images began as a series of rough sketches, small and scribbly and done rapidly with a cheap ballpoint on A4 copy paper. A set of coloured pencil drawings followed more slowly, employing compasses and a ruler, and a more credible pad of cartridge paper.

The images were carefully composed, with clarity and uniformity of design being prominent requirements on the artist's list of priorities. Each figure is posed according to the Symbol's traditional attribution: all the Fixed Zodiacal signs are enthroned, the Cardinals are moving to their right, and the Mutable Signs are depicted moving to the left and looking in the opposite direction. (The Court cards follow a similar protocol, the Knights standing full-face, the Queens enthroned, and the Pages seemingly undecided, going one way and pausing to glance back. The suit cards are deliberately simple and uniform, the intention being to illustrate the principle rather than to exhibit any talent.) The Planetary figures are all facing out of their cards with the exception of the Moon. The four Elemental figures are moving from left to right and are not delineated in quite the same fashion as everyone else; they do not carry anything for they embody their Element and are their own Weapons. The tones of colour are those most usually associated with each attribution, and the majority of the weapons held by the different figures are also chosen according to tradition.

Finally, after designing the frames and the lettering, the preparatory drafts were translated into watercolour paintings. The name of the attributed Symbol and the value of the English letter assigned thereto appears at the bottom of the card. The traditional title appears at the top, thus allowing the designs to assume their intended context. All but one of the Trumps is characterised with a representative figure, the exception being that attributed to Pisces, which bears a depiction of the Fishes.

The 26 illustrations combine English Qaballistic interpretation and traditional symbolic motifs, and are constructed with simplicity and consistency of design throughout the 26. Now we will describe the pictures given to the artist, with some explanations of the imagery, in the accustomed order.

1. **THE FOOL** is the Title of the card attributed to Air. The Element is nebulous, with little or no mass to offset the lightness of its substance; its nature is buoyant and floaty and also penetrating into every space, as the Fool's wit surrounds the Court and touches all with the precision of his analysis while he remains aloof. His chameleon character is his protection, and his wisdom is his guide as he negotiates his path; he knows with certainty that he cannot make a false step. The figure is seen from below, as if he is floating up and away from the viewer; he wears the Fool's three-pointed cap with bells. The symbol of Air, the upright triangle with a horizontal bar, is shaded with tones of pale yellow which is the colour traditionally given to the Element, and the figure is perhaps wearing a skin-tight costume, or body paint, in the complementary hues of purple and also pale sky-blue.

2. The card attributed to Mercury has been called The Magician: but we needed that title for the Uranus card and so we returned to an earlier title of this Trump, **THE JUGGLER**. There was a short debate about choosing another title altogether, "Messenger" and "Priest" came under

consideration, the former for the mythological associations of Mercury, and the latter because PRIEST=MERCURY=115 by E.Q. It was decided to remain as near to the old system as possible, for the sake of clarity and context, and to give the figure the winged sandals and herald's wand appropriate to Mercury, with shaven head and left hand raised in blessing appropriate to his priestly qualities. The figure wears a simple tunic which leaves room for doubt as to sexual orientation since the deity is hermaphroditic tending towards the masculine. The youthful face is not entirely trustworthy, as befits the Patron of Thieves. The inference is that this character juggles his messages with logic and counter-arguments that bedazzle to conceal. The colouring is predominantly orange and purple in accordance with Western esoteric tradition.

3. The third card in the 22-letter system is called THE PRIESTESS or "High Priestess" and attributed to the Moon. The lunar cycle is the primary source of a woman's power and magic, and the title is thus indisputable. *Liber AL* gives the unqualified rank and therefore so do we. The Priestess does not have to look like a woman in holy orders, neither does she have to be enthroned. That state is more static than dynamic, and astrologically the Moon is the fastest mover of the celestial bodies and constantly changing her appearance. Thus the idea which informed the image was of a young girl with a dressing up box, trying on a bridal costume. The decoration on the dress recalls the many breasts of Diana. One of the most obvious Lunar Weapons is the Mirror she holds in her left hand; in which we can see a face, perhaps that of the figure, or perhaps the glass is angled so as to reflect the viewer. This is the only

figure whose back is turned to the viewer, suggestive of the secrecy and concealment periodically enjoyed by this character. The colours are predominantly pale grey-blue to lilac-purple to indicate the Moon, with splashes of red for the monthly flux and other blood-lettings.

4. Venus, the Supreme Goddess of Beauty and Love, is indubitably THE EMPRESS. She is depicted in the usual manner, as a beautiful naked Woman, stepping forth like a model. Her headdress is of myrtle and red roses, and her right hand is adjusting the Girdle, one of the traditional Weapons of Venus. It is for the viewer to decide whether she is loosening or securing the fastening. The colours are all appropriate to Her, shades of emerald-green and honey-amber and rosy-pink.

5. The fifth card in the 22-letter system is THE EMPEROR, attributed to Aries. Aries is the first Sign of the Zodiac, the Eastern Cardinal point and place of dawn from whence the Sun, Moon, and Stars, all rise. Aries is therefore associated with birth and initiation; moreover, ARIES=BABE=66 in E.Q. Juxtaposing these ideas with the notion of an Emperor we see the small child who would rule absolute, dominating the household with obstinate tyranny. The image therefore is of a toddler taking its first steps, the right hand reaching for whatever has captured the attention in the moment, the Weapon in the left hand already half forgotten. It is a Burin, an engraving tool for making permanent marks upon stone or metal, as the advent of a baby makes a permanent mark upon its environment. The colours are the oranges and reds appropriate to Sign and Title.

6. The Sign of Taurus the Bull is associated with the sixth card, **THE HIEROPHANT**. The Hierophant is the Keeper of the Mysteries who transmits and interprets the ancient wisdom for his people. He is rather mysterious himself and sometimes has a little half-smile. Taurus rules the second House, signifying the possessions and property in the Astrological chart; in this instance the ownership is concerned with spiritual rather than temporal qualities. Synthesising these two sets of ideas we find a figure holding a precious casket which contains the Mystery. Rich jewellery is worn and a belt which recalls the Girdle of Venus, for Venus rules Taurus; the casket is studded with emeralds to emphasis the beauty and truth of the Goddess in the character of the Hierophant. The figure is strongly built and has the head of a Bull which may recall other bull-headed entities to contribute to the viewer's understanding; and enthroned, a situation more static than dynamic as befits the earthy nature and Fixed quality of the Sign. The colours are similar to those used for the Empress card but leaning towards more earthy shades of green and brown, with the royal blue-purple hues to suggest the richness associated with kings.

7. The sequence of Zodiacal attribution continues with **THE LOVERS** and Gemini, the Sign of the Heavenly Twins. The two figures are mirror images and perhaps genderless, or merely adolescent. Their embrace may be in friendship or in conflict; it is left for the viewer to decide. The colours are orange, magenta-purples and pale blue-greys appropriate to the Sign, its Ruler (Mercury) and its elemental quality (Air).

8. The attribution of **THE CHARIOT** to the Sign of Cancer at first seems an awkward juxtaposition, for Cancer is the Sign of the Mother and the Home and prefers stability, and the Chariot is a carriage designed for war and rapid transportation. The clue is in the traditional concealment of the Charioteer's face, for the Womb of the Mother is the Chariot and the face of the unborn child is hidden as it rides therein. Therefore the figure is of a pregnant Woman, her right hand resting upon her swollen belly. The Weapon she holds in her left hand is a Key, a symbol of Hecate as Cancer is the North Cardinal point of midnight; moreover KEY=MOON=49 by E.Q., the Moon being the ruler of the Sign. This Key may also unlock the Hierophant's casket. The colours are the pinkish-browns one might find in a sea shell, and shades of blue-green and purple suggesting the ocean and the Moon.

9. The ninth card in the 22-letter system is called **JUSTICE** and Libra (the Scales) is the Sign of traditional association. Our figure is stepping carefully as if on tiptoes, or on a high-wire, maintaining equilibrium and the balance of the Scales held in the right hand regardless of the drapery that swathes the petite body and covers her head completely. The colours are the pale greens and blues appropriate to the Sign.

10. The attribution of Virgo, the Virgin of the Zodiac, to the card entitled **THE HERMIT**, does not suggest an old anchorite so much as a veiled woman, concealing her feminine mystery. The figure is adjusting her veil as she looks back, holding her sheaf of wheat boldly aloft in her left hand as if it would illuminate her way. She is dressed in

the traditional blue robes of the Virgin, and seems skittish, perhaps even nervous. The other colours are the earthy browns and greens of the Sign.

11. With the eleventh card we reach the halfway point of the 22-letter system, and it is THE WHEEL OF FORTUNE, assigned to Jupiter. Experienced astrologers will know that Jupiter, the Ruler of wealth and prosperity, is appropriately unreliable when it comes to bestowing monetary fortune. Yet he is also the God of harmonious expansion and perfected form; therefore the artist has depicted the Wheel in the horizontal plane to recall the Arthurian Round Table, giving it twelve spokes to remind the viewer of the Zodiac and other such useful divisions of the Circle. His costume design is loosely derived from the Elizabethan Renaissance, and his crown is reminiscent of those in the Hindu pantheon; the colours are predominantly royal blues and purples and yellow-gold.

12. STRENGTH is the Title given to the next card and its attributed Sign is Leo. The traditional image is that of a Woman leading a Lion, or holding the nose and mouth of the animal. Following the design protocol for Fixed Signs, the artist has the Woman enthroned; she is naked, her flaming hair tumbles like a lion's mane over her shoulders, and one foot is raised upon the toes in a coquettish pose, for She is Babalon. She gazes intently into the Lion's eyes as she opens its mouth, and the Lion turns its head to stare back at her in a passionate unspoken communion. The colours are the tawny red-gold hues of the Sign and the royal blues of Kingship.

13. The card entitled THE HANGED MAN presented the first subject for serious debate, for it is usually attributed to the Element of Water and interpreted as sacrificial in nature. Yet Water is predominantly feminine and containing and giving, nurturing and sustaining and supporting. Certainly, an overabundance of these qualities may result in causing a smothering suffocating or strangulating demise, but that is an extreme case rather than an archetypal emblem, and the association of Water with the image of a hanged man, either lawfully executed or murdered, is somewhat ugly. The emphasis is on the suffering endured in sacrifice, with shadows of sin and shame; whereas the watery symbolism tends more towards the unconditional dynamic love that is the power involved in such a ritual act. Dividing the image from the accustomed Elemental attribution and considering the concept of the Hanged Man in isolation, we see that sacrifice is merely the transmission of energy from one plane or state of existence to another, and as such it is a vital factor in the continuity of Creation. The "Spirit" is sacrificed upon the "Cross of Matter" and that is just how things are arranged, out of necessity, without Grace and without Guilt. In human terms, the physical body is the material which the "Spirit" inhabits as an individuated "Soul", or spark of consciousness, or what you will. It follows that this transference into the physical domain is concomitant with birth, and that the Hanged Man symbol has more in common with the Earth Element than with the Water Element. Earth also nurtures and sustains and supports, but moreover it really does continuously sacrifice itself to do so. When we remember that BABE=EARTH=66 by E.Q. and that human babies are generally upside down and attached to a cord at

birth, the image made by the artist is readily understood. The circular cell or womb surrounding the unborn child is positioned over the horizontal bar of the downward Earth triangle to emphasise the crossing from one state to another; the cord is inferred rather than obvious, and the sex is not determinable. The colours are those traditionally associated with Earth, and variant hues.

14. The Sign of Scorpio is appropriately attributed to the card entitled **DEATH**. The figure is a skeleton partly covered in living flesh, seated in an attitude of readiness. It is female and holds a knife in the right hand and an hourglass in the left. A drop of blood falls from the clean blade, and the hourglass is held at an angle to suggest some deception in Time. The artist agrees that it is a rather disturbing, unpleasant and visceral image, for we do not know what the living skeleton figure is about to do, where the blood has come from, and why the passage of time is being measured in such a fashion. The colours are the bright red and black and beetle-green appropriate to the Sign, and hues associated with putrefaction, with blood, and with bone.

15. The 15th card of the 22-letter system, usually called "Temperance" was renamed **ART** by Aleister Crowley, and we have adopted the latter Title as being more appropriate to the symbolism of the Sign, Sagittarius – which has little to do with abstinence and restraint. The artistic process at a basic level may be described as utilising one thing (e.g. pigment, or the edge of a chisel) in close combination with another thing (e.g. a surface) to produce a third thing (a mark) which is an expression of some facet of the artist's being. In the case of the creature represented by the Sign,

FINDING NEW SYMBOLS

man and beast are mingled to produce the third form of the Centaur. He is the personification of the Alchemical Art, by which base lead is subjected to various compounds and refinements to become pure gold. The artist has depicted him walking forwards with self-conscious purpose, and turning to his right to look elsewhere, since this is one of the Mutable Signs of the Zodiac. The colouration of the equine portions of his body indicate his purity. He has a nonchalant beauty which he proudly demonstrates in the confidence with which he holds both bow and arrow ready for use in his left hand; his traditional Weapon is the Aimed Arrow. The other colours are the two primaries yellow and blue, and the green that comes from mixing them.

16. The attribution of Capricorn the Goat to the card entitled THE DEVIL betrays a misunderstanding of the Zodiac Sign. Capricorn is the Sign of Midwinter; when the Sun enters here at the Solstice we know that the rebirth of the year is approaching with lengthening daytime and warmer temperatures. The figure is posed in the Sign of Osiris Risen and holds the Phoenix Wand in the right hand to re-emphasise the symbolism of rebirth. He has an elongated goat-like face and goat's horns, one of which is broken in the traditional manner. His torso and legs are wreathed in ivy to recall the restriction associated with the traditional image; the plant is sacred to the season. We leave it to the viewer to form other correspondences with this particular time of year. The colouring is black and grey and tones of indigo and crimson.

17. The next card has been called "The House of God" and "The Tower Struck Down" and is attributed to Mars.

Although we are familiar with the alchemical mystery usually signified by this card, in the present context we find it is less relevant than the energy which drives it, symbolised by Mars. We have therefore assigned the Title THE TOWER which is a more open-ended description of the quality of the card. The figure's armour is loosely derived from the Roman pattern. He looks a bit battered and dirty as if he has come from some arena of physical labour, for Mars is simply raw energy and although he tends easily towards destruction His force may be harnessed and used constructively. He carries a Chain, one of the traditional Weapons of Mars, which is a significant piece of engineering equipment as well as a device of enslavement. He is pointing straight out of the card at the viewer to suggest that the choice of employment is theirs to make; YOU=MARS=39 by E.Q. We may infer that since the Tower has already been struck down, the task at hand is to rebuild it. The colours are the red and orange commonly associated with Mars.

18. Aquarius is the Zodiac Sign of the eighteenth card of the 22-letter system, and the given Title is THE STAR. In the Zodiacal life-cycle it is Aquarius that carries the Light from Capricorn when the spirit/soul begins to be individuated, to Pisces where it swims like a primordial fish in the pre-birth environment. In E.Qaballistic terms AQUARIUS=95 =THE STAR, which is a clear enough correspondence; and WATER=A LIGHT. The character of Aquarius is therefore seen as bearing Water which has the quality of a Light. The usual mythological attribution is Ganymede, the handsome youth who was immortalized as the Cup-Bearer of the Gods on account of his physical

beauty, but our synthesis suggests a different image, for "Light-Bearer" is one of the Titles of Lucifer. He is also called the Morning Star; and thus the refulgent beauty of Venus at dawn accounts for Ganymede. The Sign is ruled by Saturn, as is its predecessor Capricorn which is often equated with Baphomet; the connection between Aquarius and Lucifer thus makes a pleasing symmetry across the Zodiac from the two saturnine winter Signs to those of high summer, Leo and Cancer, ruled by the Sun and the Moon. The Water-bearer is the Light-bearer (AQUARIUS=BEARER=95) and accordingly the figure is depicted with the horns, pointy ears, bat-wings, and cloven hoof associated with Lucifer. The vessel is pouring forth light as he looks on with an expression of mischievous pleasure and surprise. The colours are the airy pale blues, greens, purples, and white appropriate to the Sign, and the complementary hues of orange and black.

19. **THE MOON** is the Title of the next card and Pisces is the Zodiacal attribution. The traditional designs feature two towers and two crescent moons and two dogs, and the card has much to do with the deceptions and illusions of the Piscean Twelfth House of Secrets. Our image has the two fishes of the Sign, and the customary pair of reflective lunar spheres, apparently existing on the same plane; and a single tower in another dimension with its reflection suspended beneath. This is the only Trump card with no figure. The dogs are omitted since they introduce a direction of emphasis to the whole symbol which in this context is inappropriate. The colours are the magenta-purple-blues, greens and pinks of the Sign.

20. **THE SUN** is of course both Title and attribution of the twentieth card of the 22-letter system. The figure is of a well-proportioned naked man, his active pose loosely based upon that of the dancing Shiva. His crown too owes something to the Hindu styling; his beard is after the fashion of Ancient Egypt; he is masked, for we cannot gaze at the brilliance that is the radiant face of the Sun. In his right hand he holds aloft a large Ankh, symbol of Life, and of Venus, and of the Going that is his function. The colours are the appropriate Solar yellows and pinks.

21. The penultimate card of the 22 has been called "The Last Judgement" but we prefer Crowley's title **THE AEON**. The attribution is the Element of Fire; in E. Q. FIRE=NUIT=78, and so the image is the shape of the Goddess bending from the black of infinite space into the starry blue within the outline of the red Fire Triangle.

22. The card assigned to Saturn, the last and slowest-moving planet visible to the human eye (under normal conditions: it is sometimes possible to see Uranus), is traditionally called "The Universe" or **THE WORLD**. We take up the latter Title for the other has implications which potentially narrow the understanding of the whole symbol in the present context. Saturn teaches patience and endurance by making things slow and difficult, astrologically he is associated with old age, and he is often depicted with the Scythe. We have excluded this very particular weapon as it brings an emphasis which is both undesirable and inappropriate. The artist has instead borrowed shamelessly from William Blake, and portrayed the deity as engaged in grinding out some substance to

a fine powder. These grains might be for the hourglass held by the figure of Death, since Saturn is traditionally associated with Time. The colours are the appropriate dull tones of grey, purple-brown, and black.

23. Now we launch into the outer reaches of the Solar System and beyond the range of unaided vision. The discovery of Uranus in 1781, in the early years of the Industrial Revolution, marked the sudden introduction of many new inventions, and all sorts of "magical" technologies. We could almost have named this card "The Inventor", or "The Alchemist", except for the restrictions which would have been imposed by such Titles; we have instead called it THE MAGICIAN which is more open-ended and appropriate to the magickal-astrological understanding of the planetary deity. As the Sky-God he frames the Earth; therefore the artist has portrayed the globe within a transparent cube which he somehow holds suspended between his hands as if he has just finished making it. The figure's costume is based on that of a typical garden gnome, with trousers tucked into boots, rolled-up sleeves, red cap, and apron; his kinship with Earth is enhanced by his E. Qaballistic value, URANUS=EARTH=66. The other colours are those commonly used by cartographers to indicate different contoured areas of terrain.

24. THE MYSTIC is the Title given to the card of Neptune. The planet was observed but not properly recognised many times before its existence and position were scientifically deduced and confirmed in 1846. While Uranus can sometimes be seen under particular circumstances without assistance, Neptune is properly invisible to the human eye,

and with his discovery came a new awareness of things hidden from view. Researches into psychoanalysis, atomic theory, comparative religious spirituality and occultism grew and gained in popularity over the subsequent 150 years. Astrologers give the deity rulership over Pisces and the Twelfth House; He is the God of the ocean depths and similar mysterious places and phenomena. He is portrayed holding the traditional fish-spear or Trident in the right hand, while a strange pearly sphere is floating in the crook of the left arm. He seems to be looking into it, but the face is obscured in shadow and we cannot be certain. The colours are all found in the sea.

25. Pluto is the outermost planetary body recognised by astrologers. Taking at least 20 years to traverse a single Zodiac Sign, his power influences whole generations at once, and causes deep-seated transformations such as have occurred worldwide since his discovery in the 1930's. He is the God of the Underworld and the Keeper of the Dead. He is portrayed holding a spray of lilies, associated with funerary rites for their strong perfume. The cow skull is a representation of the Cap or Helmet of Invisibility from the Greek myths of Hades. We could have named him "The Watcher" or even "The Headless One" but after much discussion we chose the Title THE THRESHOLD as being suitably open-ended for interpretation. The colours are tones of grey and dark blue and black, and white, all appropriate for the last adventure of death and transformation, and red for the tendency towards violence which is a hallmark of Pluto. At the edge of the Solar System it represents a point of no return. The depiction is unique in the set of 26 in that the figure can only be seen through the symbols upon the card.

26. In this sequence the final card signifies the expanse of deep space and is attributed to the Element of Water. The crowned and bejewelled female figure seems to be rising from the blue depth of the Water Triangle. She is called THE CONCUBINE for it is the nature of the Element to give unconditionally and unreservedly; She may be identified with Babalon, since CUP=56 and 65=WATER=BABALON=WISDOM. Her giving is her reward, here there is no sacrifice, only love for love's sake. Her hands are raised in a gesture which allows different interpretations, for Her Love is beguiling and tempting as well as endlessly bestowed. The colours are tones of blue, and the complementary hue, orange.

THEORY OF DIVINATION

A divinatory system is a set of symbolic representations of factors existing in the Universe which have a discernible influence on human affairs. As the Universe is infinite, containing an infinite number of such factors, a certain amount of generalisation and conflation of symbols is necessary in order to maintain a sensible and practical number of component parts in the divinatory set. The divination consists of a given number of these component parts which are separated from the set and taken to represent the particular forces at work in a given situation, at that moment in time. The accuracy of the divination is partly dependent upon the interpretive skills of the operator, and partly upon the component parts in the set, for the greater the number and variety of factors delineated the more details may be obtained in a selection therefrom; and yet too much data may be impossible to process and synthesise into a single complete interpretation.

The horary astrologer takes the divinatory set that is presented in the moment by the positions of stars and planets as seen from his location on the Earth, drawing up the chart at the time of asking the question. Operators of other systems carry their symbolic cosmology with them in various forms such as cards, coins, bones, shells, stones, sticks, or other sets of items that are recognised by the operator as representing facets of reality. The casting of the divination assumes a coherence in the scheme of the Universe by which everything is connected in Time to everything else and all events are prescient; this happens in a non-spatial dimension that is accessed by the operator through the component parts of the divination which present a snap-shot of the moment as the casting is made.

TRADITIONAL TAROT

The Tarot has come to the 21st Century more or less fixed to the Hebrew Tree of Life, the 22 major component parts (the Trump cards) having been aligned with the 22 letter symbols of the Kabbalists in an attempt to produce a really complete portrait of reality. The system works, in its own terms; but there are factors in modern human consciousness which were apparently unknown in earlier historical times. Occultists of any stripe in the 21st Century have knowledge of the universe which includes three outer planets beyond the visible wandering stars observed by their predecessors, and a different vision of the planet on which they live from any which could have been experienced before in recorded history. The correspondences traced by the occult revivalists are no longer entirely satisfactory, as their logic has been overtaken by technology, by academic investigation, and by social change. Another important new factor is of course the advent of the English Qaballa, one of the most significant developments in the post-revival reformation of Occultism. English Qaballa allows infinite correspondences with symbol-numbers that are derived from words written with English letters, using the Lexicon of *Liber AL vel Legis* as the foundation of the system and with the Complete Tree of Life at its core; and thus every system known to humanity and expressed in English is capable of finding some parallel with E. Qaballistic magickal philosophy and ritual.

E. QABALLISTIC CARTOMANCY

The Complete Tree of Life is a template of reality in twenty-eight pieces, according to E.Q. For the purpose of cartomantic divination these are correlated with traditional esoteric principles as follows: 12 Zodiac signs, 10 planets, and 4 Elements, each symbol having its corresponding English letter and numeric value; the remaining pair represent the microcosmic magical/spiritual identity (Soul) of the operator, and whatever conception the operator allows of the spiritual/divine macrocosm, the eternal infinite existence (Creator). The latter has no imagery and is placed in the position of the Perfect Tiphareth as the source and centre of pure harmony, while the former is ascribed to the sphere immediately above Kether in Manifestation; the three dots of the Zero Trigram are the only image upon this card. The other twenty-six Trigrams correspond with the English Alphabetical letters, we willl presently show. (See Diagram 4, page 177).

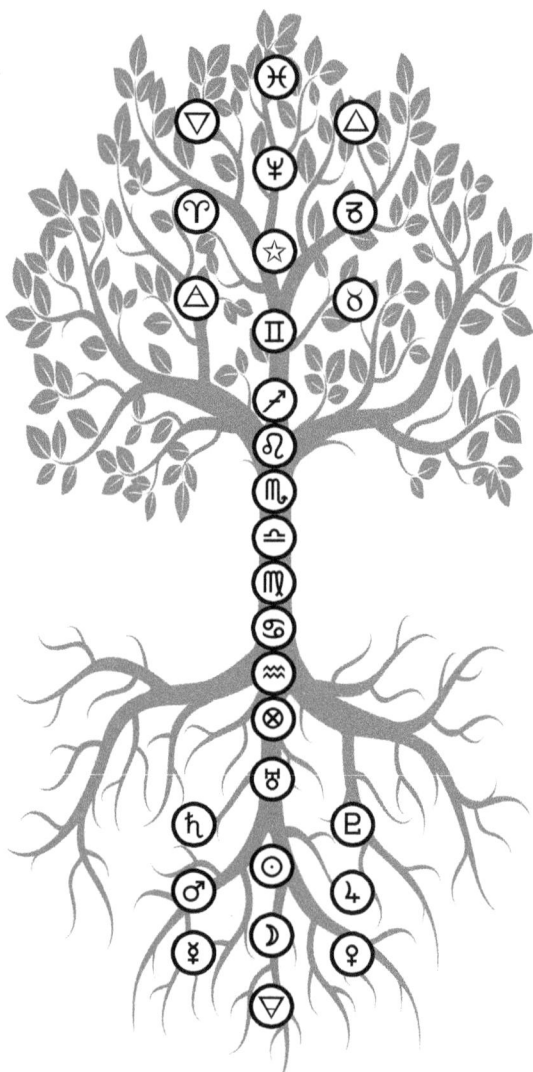

DIAGRAM 3: THE CORRESPONDENCES OF THE ENGLISH QABALLISTIC TAROT ON THE COMPLETE TREE OF LIFE.

FINDING NEW SYMBOLS

A year was spent working with an E.Q. Tarot deck, experimenting with divinatory techniques and interpretations; the most useful results are given here.

Methods of casting the cards will vary according to the operator's choice, the number of cards drawn and the placement of them upon the table is not dyed in stone, and therefore we share our techniques only to offer some suggestions.

The first action is always to shuffle the pack, concentrating upon the question to be answered. Our first question is usually concerning the divination itself – do we have permission to ask, will we receive unequivocal answers? We will shuffle the cards twice and then cut for an answer. The cards can be roughly divided into positive and negative, so if we cut to the Ace of Cups we have a definite affirmative, but if we get the nine of Swords we will put the cards away without further ado, and await a more auspicious time. This demonstrates respect and consideration for the Guardian Spirit of the Tarot, with whom it is desirable to be on good terms.

Having got the "all clear" we will shuffle again, all the while concentrating on the question and repeating it, and we will state how many shuffles are to be performed before casting the cards. "This is my question, I will shuffle three times and then lay out the cards." Sometimes a card will drop during the shuffling, this is usually of significance and may provide the answer. There should be some attempt at analysis before deciding whether to continue. The card being replaced, the shuffling begins once more, stating how many times, and concentrating on the question as before.

In the case of a divination for a Querent, we will say that our work is on behalf of another, and when satisfied with the shuffle we will place the pack face down upon the table for the Querent to cut the pack, while concentrating on their question. We then cast the spread from the top card of the Querent's cut.

The correspondences with the Complete Tree have made possible the synthesis of astrological theory and the 27 Yi Ching Trigrams noted by Crowley in the Class A publication *Liber Trigrammaton sub figura XXVII*. We have researched two different methods of casting the cards which reflect these divinatory systems, apart from the usual ten-card spread, and the simple cutting of a single card. (This can turn into a sort of conversation if one asks for clarification and further details; unless one wants permission for follow-up questions the pack should not be shuffled in between, just squared up and put back on the table; and if one finds the same card coming up repeatedly this usually means that the conversation is over, or the question must be rephrased. For instance, when the same card is the answer to both taking a course of action, and not doing so, asking about the nature and characteristics of the most beneficial course of action may produce a more definitive answer.)

<small>Astrological Casting</small>

Twelve cards are laid face up on the table. Each card corresponds to one of the twelve astrological Houses, and so the spread is usefully (but not necessarily) laid out as a clock-face, beginning with a card at the 9 o'clock position (the First House). Working anti-clockwise as if drawing a chart in the usual way, lay a second card at the 8 o'clock position, a third card at the 7 o'clock position, a fourth at 6 o'clock, and so on round the circle. Whether each card is placed radially, or arranged in four groups of three beginning with the first card (followed by the second and third cards), the fourth card (followed by the fifth and sixth), the seventh (followed by the 8th and 9th), and the tenth (followed by the 11th and 12th) cards, is a matter of choice for the easiest reading. The twelve cards are interpreted according to their astrological House positions, and the weight of the elemental influences upon the moment are discerned from the corresponding Triplicities (Cardinal, Fixed, or Mutable) and Quaternaries (Fire, Earth, Air, and Water).

The Cardinal card positions (1st, 4th, 7th, and 10th) show characteristics of influences in their first beginning strengths. The Fixed card positions (2nd, 5th, 8th, and 11th) show the established influences in the matter. The Mutable card positions (3rd, 6th, 9th, and 12th) show the typical characteristics of influences that are changeable or being altered in the matter. These groups of cards can be seen as patterns of squares or crosses in the spread.

The Quaternals or Elemental card positions can be seen as triangular formations in the spread, each containing a cardinal, a fixed, and a mutable position. The Fire Triangle (1st, 5th, and 9th) shows the workings of all things Fiery in the spread; the emotional dynamic; impulses, enthusiasms, pressures, activations, and passions. The Earth Triangle (2nd, 6th, and 10th) shows the influences of the Earthy Element in the spread; the material dynamic; the energies of holding and possessing and strengthening and fortifying and solidifying. The Air Triangle (3rd, 7th, and 11th) shows the intellectual dynamic; the mental energies whether inwardly destructive or outwardly constructive, the processes of negotiating with the matter at hand, and the hopes, ambitions, and certainties of the Querent. The Water Triangle (4th, 8th, and 12th) shows the temporal dynamic, the flow and rhythm of time though the spread; the result or conclusion, the background processes of reaching the answer, the secret or hidden areas of the matter: deceptions and enemies and force majeure are discernible here.

The first card has the characteristic of Cardinal Fire and represents the Querent. The second is characterised by Fixed Earth, and is the portion of the question that is owned by the Querent, the Querent's status in the matter (material or otherwise), the "chips in hand". The third card with the characteristic of Mutable Air represents the mental state of the Querent and shows what kinds of communications are involved in the matter. The 4th card has the characteristic of Cardinal Water and is the homecoming or resolution of the matter; if the Two of Disks is found here the status quo of the spread will soon be altered by an event affecting the parameters of the question so as almost to nullify the interpretation. The 5th card, characterised by Fixed Fire, shows whatever the Querent is risking, or playing with, or gambling; this is the portion of the question that is (at least potentially) pleasing or enjoyable. The 6th card with the characteristic of Mutable Earth represents all that will assist the Querent in the matter, whether as the health and fitness of the Querent or as people who will be helpful. The seventh card is characterised by Cardinal Air and represents the Question itself, the immediate opposition or the cause that

FINDING NEW SYMBOLS

has impelled the divination, whatever is "coming at" the Querent. The card in the 8th position has the characteristic of Fixed Water and indicates the transformational portion of the matter over which the Querent has no control; the changes that are required for the result may be discerned here. The 9th card, characterised by Mutable Fire, shows a wide-angle view of the matter and its effect in the longer term; the spiritual portion and philosophical impact of the situation may be interpreted here; also journeys and long distances, should these be involved. The card in the 10th position has the characteristic of Cardinal Earth and represents the ruling influence or the seat of authority in the matter. The 11th card has the characteristic of Fixed Air and will show the reliability or uncertainty of assumptions, hopes, and fears, about all aspects of the matter. The characteristic of Mutable Water is embodied at the 12th position, and the card found here represents the mysterious and secret forces involved in the fated moments of asking the Question and casting the spread.

This astrologically derived cartomantic technique will give a precise but rather static overview of a situation and the strengths, weaknesses, assistances or hindrances involved; accurate predictions of future events may be more difficult, depending on the nature of the question, because this casting has no moving parts as are used in Horary Astrology to project events forward in time.

YI CHING CASTING

Three cards are laid face up in a line. These represent firstly, the Yin, secondly, the Yang, and thirdly, the Tao of the matter at hand; as it were the source, the shape, and the manifestation. A second line of three cards is laid out, either above or below the first according to choice. Now the first line is read as Yin of Yin, Yin of Yang, and Yin of Tao, three resonances of the source and energy of the matter. The second line is Yang of Yin, Yang, and Tao, three resonances of the shape and form of the matter. A third line of three cards is laid out, representing the Tao of the Yin, the Tao of the Yang, and the Tao of the Tao, three resonances of the manifested result. The nine cards together give a description of the question and the answer. The change that one can make is to put the first six cards to the bottom of the pack, and keeping the Tao line as the Yin of the next casting, lay out two new lines. This is useful when the divination concerns a set of circumstances which the Querent wishes to influence; however, it is important to note that this is a magical procedure which can only be done once with each nine-card spread: the Tao line cannot be changed a second time, and we advise due diligence of forethought before commencing such an operation.

Suggested Interpretations

We do not differentiate between cards according to their orientation; in our experiments we found that a sufficiently accurate reading depends not so much on whether a card is reversed or not as on its relationship with the rest of the spread. In the English Qaballistic philosophy nothing happens in isolation; the Tarot deck represents an organic wholistic and inclusive reality, and a selection of pieces from the whole continue to act together in one spread. For example, any card in the suit of Swords will be slightly dignified by the presence of the Ace of Swords, by the suit

Court cards or by the Trumps of The Fool and Justice; and if it is one of the malevolent Sword cards then the finer qualities of these other cards will be somewhat distorted; but in the absence of other Swords and with cards in the suit of Disks or Cups the edge will be blunted for it will have no other symbol to connect with in the spread; unless two or more cards of the same number appear, which will indicate a predominant manifested condition of Elemental energy. The presence of more martial Trumps such as the Tower or the Emperor could add to the detrimental effect, and so forth; much more could be written, but it must suffice to commend the effect of one card upon another as an interesting study in E. Qaballistic cartomancy.

The appropriate stanza from *Liber XXVII* is included as part of the description of the Trump cards. Some have been changed slightly for the sake of grammar. The curious language provokes a deeper comprehension of the symbolism of each card; we include our own short interpretation of each to explain this. The meanings of the Trumps are given in the order of the English Qaballistic Alphabet, and the numbering of the Trigrams according to *Liber XXVII* appears in Roman numerals. These remarks are taken from the analysis of the divinatory properties of the correspondences we have explored previously, and are a focussed interpretation of our work with *Liber AL* II:76.

T<small>HE BLANK CARD</small>.

FINDING NEW SYMBOLS

This card is an empty frame and represents that power in the Universe with which the operator is communicating through the medium of the Tarot pack. Names, attributes, images and symbols of the consciousness that is greater than one's own are necessarily very personal, and therefore it seemed most appropriate to offer the operator the choice of adding their own design, or not. Drawing this card is an indication of force majeure, divine providence, destiny, and so on; "the Universe is watching and all is as it should be, whether you approve or not." Generally this is a benefic card, but it may also indicate that there is nothing that can be done to influence the course of events.

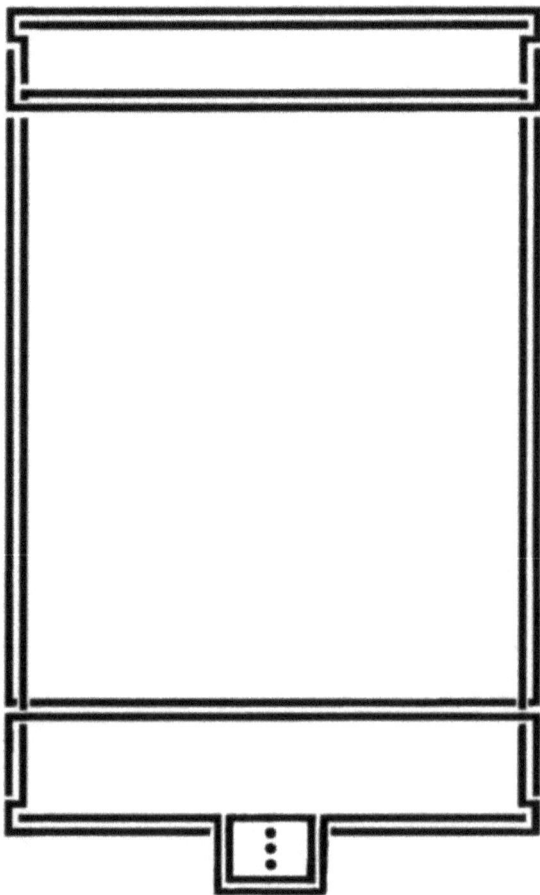

FINDING NEW SYMBOLS

This card has the multiple frame used throughout the rest of the pack. The three dots of the Trigram are at the bottom and the rest of the card is again left blank for the operator's personal choice, for here is represented the operator's magical will, the energised individual consciousness engaged in the communication with the rest of the Universe through the medium of the Tarot pack. Drawing this card shows that the matter is in the hand of the querent. This is usually a fortunate card.

Liber XXVII: The Zero Trigram.

"Here is Nothing under its three forms. It is not, yet informeth all things."

(The dimension of Not-being existing in space-time.)

"Death"

1. Scorpio

Unexpected and unpleasant change, catastrophe, betrayal. An unlooked-for turn of events. Bad news. The arrival of an uninvited guest. The cuspal moment of breakage, evolutionary chance, a watershed moment, necessary and inevitable change. A twist of Fate for good or ill, usually the latter. This is nearly always an unfortunate card.

Liber XXVII: Trigram v. 1=A

"...The Imperfection became manifest, presiding over the fading of perfection."

(The first alteration in Nothing is the Death of Not-being.)

FINDING NEW SYMBOLS

The pressure of the aimed arrow between bowstave and string. Force applied to form so as to redefine its shape. A concealment which does not entirely hide but reveals particular details. A process of change that is partly obscured from view. The combining of two principles to produce a third principle. Refinement. A state of transition. A mixing or blending of forces and forms. Potential, existing in two worlds at once. There is grace rather than malice in this card.

Liber XXVII: Trigram vi. 2=L
"The Woman arose, veiling the Upper Heavens with Her Body of Stars."
(The transition from Nothing into Less-Than-Nothing.)

THE DEVIL

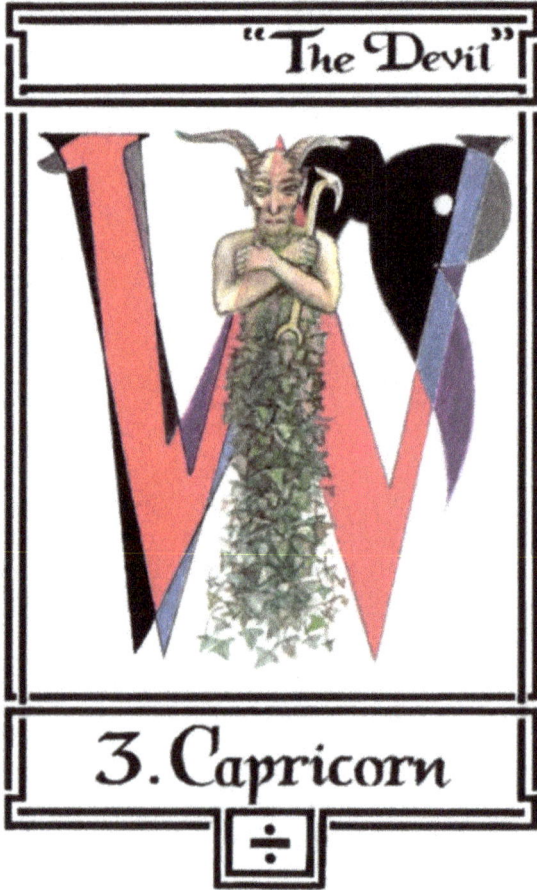

"The Devil"

3. Capricorn

÷

FINDING NEW SYMBOLS

The recognition of what is and what is not. The defining of duality by a third stabilising factor. Life observing Now in Time. The definition in three dimensions of the duality formed by the first imperfection. The whole calculation of 0=2. The tendency towards stability that is a limiting factor. A person with fixed ideas. Dogmatism. Clinging to a particular point of view. Duty. A turgid situation. Progress impeded by tangled difficulties. This card can also indicate the cutting of such bonds, a reawakening and rejuvenation, a realisation of plans, an arrival; or the brief opportunity for these.

Liber XXVII: Trigram iii. 3=W
"The purity divided by Strength, the Force of the Demiurge."
(The acceptance of the Division for love's sake.)

"The Wheel of Fortune"

4. Jupiter

FINDING NEW SYMBOLS

The vanishing point of probability. The perfect origin of design; an accurate plan; the requirement of change and the attending hope of good fortune. Pure chance. A momentary stability. The throwing of the dice. The point of no return. The moment made perfect which cannot last. The temptation of "What if?" Most often a fortunate card indicating a portion of good luck, but not to be relied upon unless other agreeable cards appear in the same reading.

Liber XXVII: Trigram xv. 4=H
"The horror of Time which perverts all things and hides the Purity with unnameable loathsomeness."

(The Manifestation of Time, and the creation of probability that is necessary for the progress of Time.)

"The Tower"

5. Mars

FINDING NEW SYMBOLS

The energy of work, physical rather than intellectual labour, force used for a purpose. A release of energy. The liberation of energy from restriction. Rapid onset of instability. Explosion. Detonation. Force unleashed from form. The moment of breakdown, the physical reaction. The recognition of fear. The adrenaline rush. Rash or reckless behaviour. Impatience. The sudden need for quick reaction and output of energy – whether physical, emotional, intellectual, or spiritual may be deduced from the question, or from other cards in the spread. This card often indicates a violent and destructive event or a dangerous situation.

Liber XXVII: Trigram xvii. 5=S

"The Black Brothers unveiled themselves and raised their heads without shame or fear."

(The revealing of raw unbound energy.)

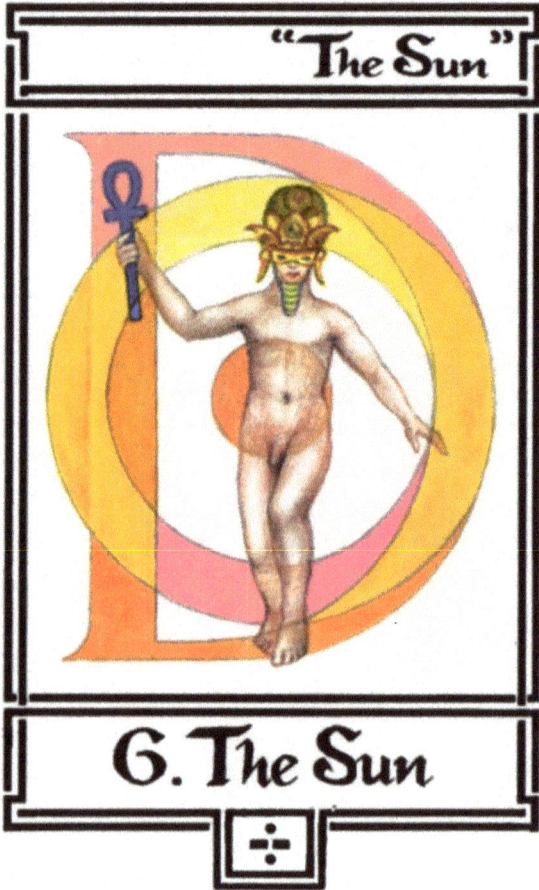

"The Sun"

6. The Sun

Equilibrium. Harmony. Balanced energy. Righteousness. Co-operation of force and form. Good government, a beneficial arrangement or association. Harmonised dynamism. Love. The returning or rewarding of love. Vitalised stability. Healthy peace. Success. Always a beneficial card.

Liber XXVII: Trigram iv. 6=D
"The Cross formulated in the Universe that as yet was not."
(The abiding presence of unrestricted Harmony.)

Sensual pleasure. Artistic inspiration; the pleasure of love. Emotional satisfaction. The sensuality of love. Emotional indulgence. Libertine romance. Generally a benefic card, but can indicate a degree of immorality.

Liber XXVII: Trigram xvi. 7=O
"Sensuality arose upon the firmament, staining the sky with storms."
(The multiplication of force into form.)

THE JUGGLER

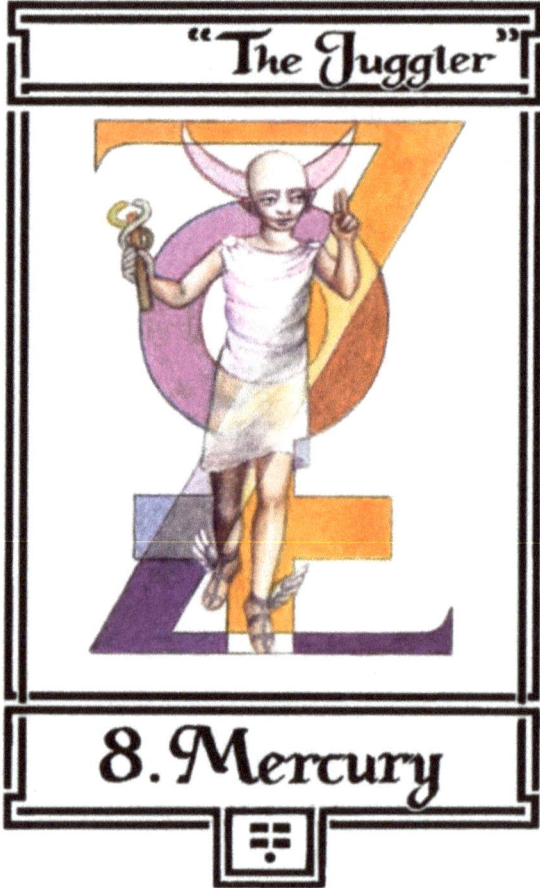

"The Juggler"

8. Mercury

Moral logic. Moral cohesion. Reasoning intellect. Question and answer. The pattern of argument. The arrangement of debate. Oratory. Rhetoric. Mental skill. Rapidity of thought. Logical analysis. The articulation of corrosion. Intellectual conflict, the experience of argument. The use of words. Reasoned evaluation of information. Falsehood juggled with honesty. Lies. Dishonesty, cheating.

Liber XXVII: Trigram xviii. 8=Z

"A soul of filth and of weakness arose and corrupted the rule of the Tao."

(The beginning of thought, and argument.)

"The Threshold"

9. Pluto

FINDING NEW SYMBOLS

The Self as an idea of the Self. The composite Self-identity. The internal mirror. The spell of self-love. The non-physical domain of the individual. The concept of the inner self. The mind of the individual as a whole unique isolated phenomena. That which formulates the "outside of the box." The synthesis of "I am" and "I am Not." Conscience. Genius. The influences upon the personality which exist beyond the normal ego-consciousness. Force Majeure. The "Recording Angel". The "Guardian Angel". The "Higher Self". A deep transformation. An awakening or expansion in consciousness. A crisis. Large scale forces or events, mob rule; a threat to the ego. This card usually threatens some inner realisation, but is not necessarily always malefic.

Liber XXVII: Trigram i. 9=K
"Now cometh the Glory of the Single One, as an imperfection and a stain."
(A glimpse of the Nothing beyond Everything.)

"The Magician"

10. Uranus

FINDING NEW SYMBOLS

A specialist, a cunning or skilled person. Private ambitions. Eccentricity. Refinement of circumstances. The individual apart from society, a considered decision to remove, progress in seclusion. Inventions. Genius. Deviousness. Obscure motivation. A surprise. A "Eureka" moment. A quick action. Radical thinking. A lightning-flash event, as of violence, or of inspiration.

Liber XXVII: Trigram xi. 10=V
"Certain secret ones concealed the Light of Purity within themselves, to protect it from persecution."
(The invention of words and images.)

"The Mystic"

11. Neptune

FINDING NEW SYMBOLS

Secrecy, concealment, and the betrayal of these. The double-cross. Falsehood, pretence for secret purposes. Underhand or deceptive behaviour. An environment of illusion. A deceived or deceptive individual. Unreliable conditions, changeable status. Mistrust. Treachery. Ambiguity. Confusion. Dream-states, clairvoyance. A situation difficult to grasp. A hidden truth. Occult forces, enchantments. This card is mysterious but not always malefic; it warns of the need for good judgement, care, and discrimination.

Liber XXVII: Trigram xiii. 11=G
"The Enemy brings confusion, concealing the light that it might be betrayed and profaned."
(The Formulation of Illusion.)

"The World"

12. Saturn

FINDING NEW SYMBOLS

Ponderous, slow, patient individual, or a condition in which these qualities prevail, or are required. Inertia. Grinding, pressing, delaying of activity. Restriction. Solidification. Crystallisation. Paralysis. Numbness. Imperceptible progress. Endurance. Slow motion. Burdensome travail which obscures the real purpose. A slowing of impetus. "Hard times." This card is sometimes dangerous to the health.

Liber XXVII: Trigram vii. 12=R

"A giant arose, of terrible strength, asserting the Spirit in a secret rite."

(Stability prevails.)

"The Priestess"

13. The Moon

The establishment of rhythmic movement. The swinging of the pendulum. A pulse. A steady beat. The rhythm of life and of existence in material form. The calibration of Time. The pattern of progress. Movement harmonised with the environment. The ebb and flow of energy, the pattern and rhythm of flux and reflux, or of inspiration and expiration. A capricious person or situation. A flirtation. Carelessness. Negligence. Inconsistent or variable conditions. A muddle.

Liber XXVII: Trigram xix. 13=C
"In the lowest corruption is form manifest, Heaven being established to bear sway."
(The rhythm of Manifestation is established.)

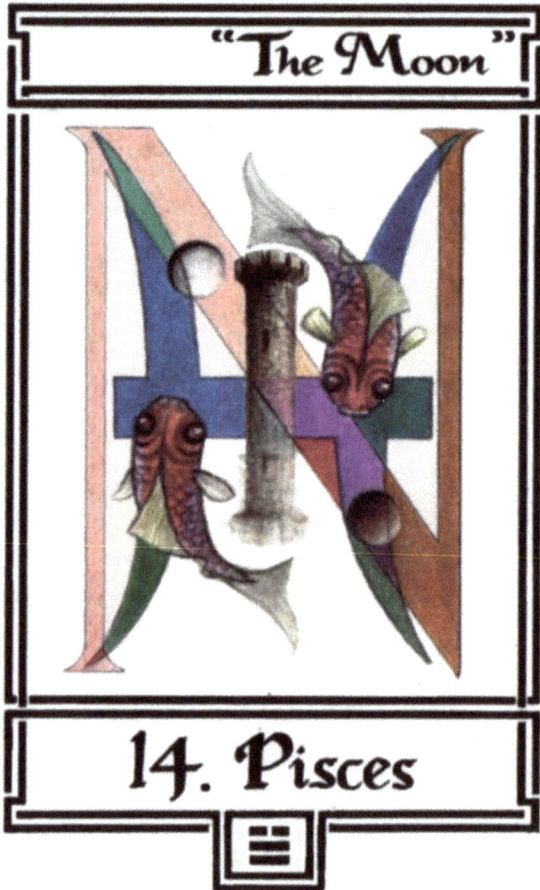

"The Moon"

14. Pisces

FINDING NEW SYMBOLS

The separation of the mutable from the insubstantial. The reflection of illusion. An illusory environment, a person subject to illusion. Instability, an unstable state. Insufficiency. The vagueness of the ethereal. Uncertain and unknown things. Clairvoyant and dreamy tendency or inclination to illusion. A person apparently out of touch with reality. Weakness. Susceptibility. A confinement. This is a potentially dangerous card.

Liber XXVII: Trigram xxii. 14=N
"The gathering of the waters from the heavens."
(Manifestation is reflected as in a mirror by the Nothingness.)

"The Star"

15. Aquarius

FINDING NEW SYMBOLS

Mischief. Harmless trickery. The attraction of confrontation. Innovative or contrary behaviour. Argument for argument's sake. Equivocation. Distraction. Temptation. Purposeless negotiation. Procrastination. Trivia. Meaningless charity. Puzzles. Unanswerable questions, amusing paradoxes. An entertainment. Originality and invention. This card sometimes warns of the necessity to give something up or to let something go to facilitate progress.

Liber XXVII: Trigram ix. 15=Y

"The Brothers of the Left-hand Path, confusing the symbols, and concealing their horror..."

(The reflection becomes Infinite Space bearing the Infinite Stars.)

THE EMPEROR

"The Emperor"

16. Aries

FINDING NEW SYMBOLS

Gentle and irresistible force, the dominance of sunrise. Initiation, first steps, new beginning. Urge. Impulse. Insistence of change. A call to arms. The command of necessity. Action without forethought. A selfish act. An oppressive individual or situation. Ambition. A risk, a prompt but ill-considered act. A tantrum. A dictatorial tyranny. Childish temper. A bully. This card often advises diplomacy.

Liber XXVII: Trigram xxi. 16=J
"Soft light."
(The Manifestation of Life.)

"The Hierophant"

17. Taurus

The act of taking possession or ownership, or the giving or conferring of ownership. Staking a claim. Proclamation of ownership as a message or sign to others. The revelation or discovery of another presence or person or situation, developing or already present. A place or a person giving or teaching information. The imparting of wisdom. A demonstration or revealing of a secret.

Liber XXVII: Trigram xxv. 17=U
"The men who began to light fires upon the earth."
(Life becomes possessed of the Mystery of Division.)

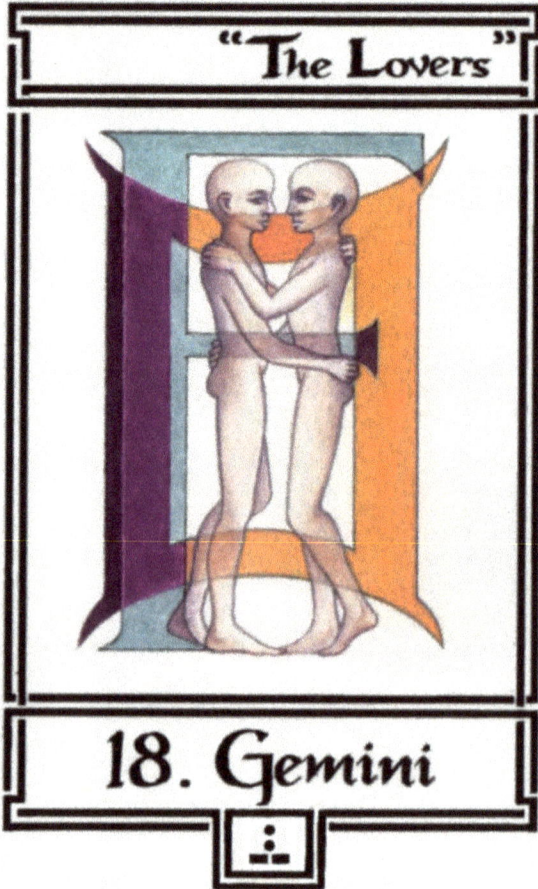

"The Lovers"

18. Gemini

FINDING NEW SYMBOLS

The harmony of mother and child. Equilibrium of birth. Creation in harmony with the creator. Reproduction in a state of balance. Life bringing forth life. The attraction of opposites. Communing or communication between two persons. A swift realisation. A partnership. A person or thing and the reflection or counterpart thereof. Division. Antagonism. A separation or a bringing together. A matched pair of opposites. A duet. A marriage, or a divorce.

Liber XXVII: Trigram ii. 18=F
"By the Weak One, the Mother, was the Glory equilibrated."
(Life united with Life.)

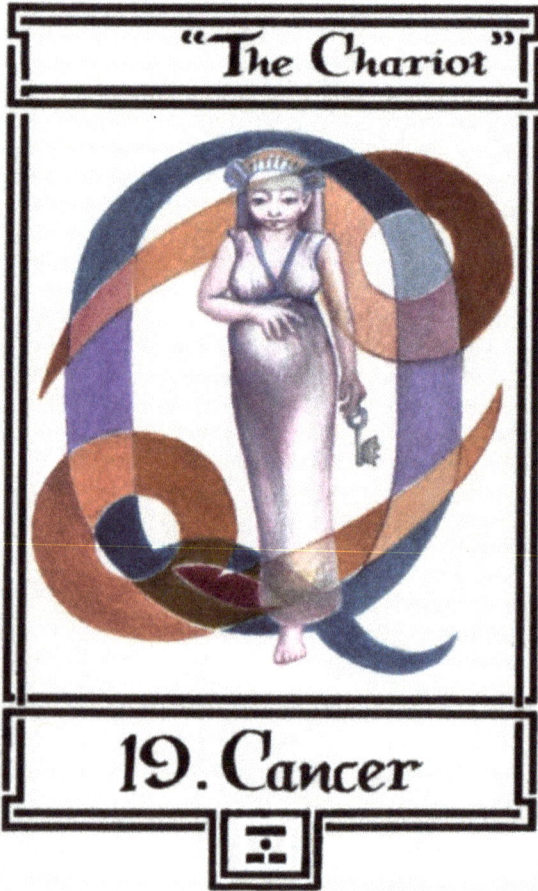

"The Chariot"

19. Cancer

Unconcealed protection. An open secret. The obvious, hidden in plain sight. The unborn child. Pregnancy. Potential. A promise. The predictable future. A known sequence of events. A clue to a mystery. Detection, deduction, inference, a solution to a problem. The perfect crime. Willingness to be deceived. Evidence withheld or ignored. Complicity. A person playing a part. An assumption. Disinformation. Pretence. A shield of ignorance. Guile. A safety which may be vulnerable or illusory. A card advising caution.

Liber XXVII: Trigram xii 19=Q
"Certain sons and daughters of Venus and of Hermes, following openly."
(Life brings forth Life.)

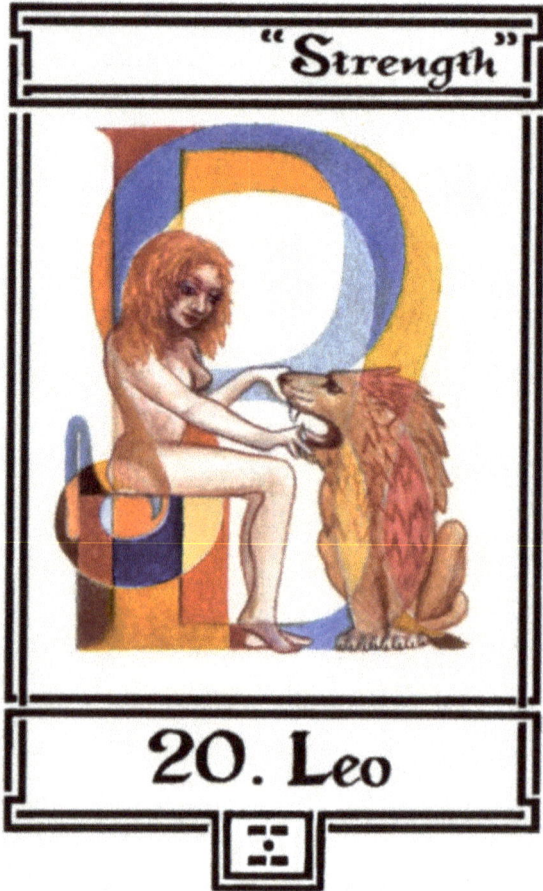

"Strength"

20. Leo

A pleasant situation or person. Good company. A meeting of minds. Romance. Passion shared. Falling in love. Friendship. An amicable gathering. Entertainment, sport, games, enjoyable activities. Singing, making music. Sharing. A celebration. A glad congregation. Harmony of body and soul. Spiritual, intellectual, emotional or physical satisfaction. Requited love. The unifying power of Love. A benefic card.

Liber XXVII: Trigram xiv. 20=B
"Certain holy nuns concealed the secret in songs upon the lyre."
(The Life was the Love of Life.)

THE HERMIT

FINDING NEW SYMBOLS

A guardian. A secret authority. A person whose source of authority is difficult to determine. A civil servant. A servant of an unknown establishment. Secret or uncertain motives. Mistrust. A dubious situation. Difficult circumstances requiring or enforcing isolation. Doubt. A variable or unreliable condition. Dissimulation. Concealed wisdom. A "guiding Light". A person who is contented with isolated circumstances. Aloofness. "Behind-the-scenes" activity. A card that warns against making assumptions.

Liber XXVII: Trigram viii. 21=M
"The Master of the Temple arose, balancing all things above the Heavens and below Earth and Hell."
(And the Love saw that it was Pure.)

"Justice"

22. Libra

FINDING NEW SYMBOLS

Judgement. A judge or a fair-minded person. Decision. Choice. The necessity of making a choice. Karma. Law. A weighing or a summing-up of evidence or factors in an argument. Casting a vote. The appointing of winners and losers. A state of temporary balance. The "calm before the storm." A necessary alteration of a situation. Stalemate. Diagnosis. Verdict. An informed opinion. Impartiality.

Liber XXVII: Trigram xx. 22=X
"The manifestation of Heaven in violent light…"
(Love accepts the impurity of Time.)

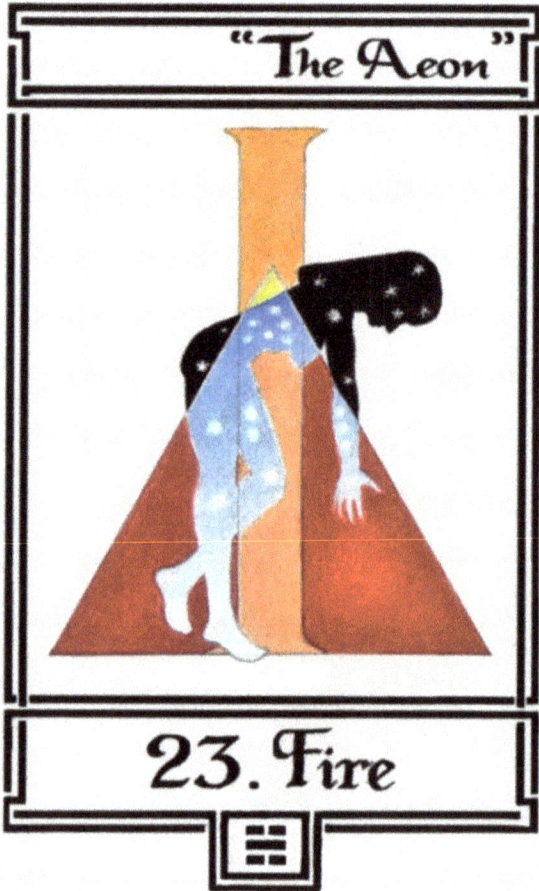

"The Aeon"

23. Fire

FINDING NEW SYMBOLS

The idea of the Self as "I". The identity of the individual. The personality. That which interacts with existence outside the self. The aspect of the self which the individual shows to the rest of the world. A forceful person. A decision, a decisive statement of self-identity and status or position. Expression of the Self in a given situation. A person taking control of a situation. "Will-power." Pressure within the individual to express the Self. Pressure of desire, the urge to express love. The feeling of love's passion.

Liber XXVII: Trigram xxiv. 23=I
"The gathering of the wide air around the globe."
(Love becomes self-aware.)

THE HANGED MAN

Disguise. A mask. The actor's make-up and costume. Putting on a disguise. An assumed identity. Playing a part. Concealment in order to achieve an objective. Voluntary transformation. Willing sacrifice. The necessity of giving up one thing in order to gain another thing. A self-appointed martyr. Transition from one state to another. The process and formula of change. Necessary or enforced change. Metamorphosis. A vulnerable state or person, or the need to protect the same. A weak start or beginning. Exposure. Convalescence. Rehabilitation. Protection. Insecurity.

Liber XXVII: Trigram x. 24=T

"The Master, as a flaming star, set a Guard of water in every Abyss."

(Love manifests in Life.)

THE CONCUBINE

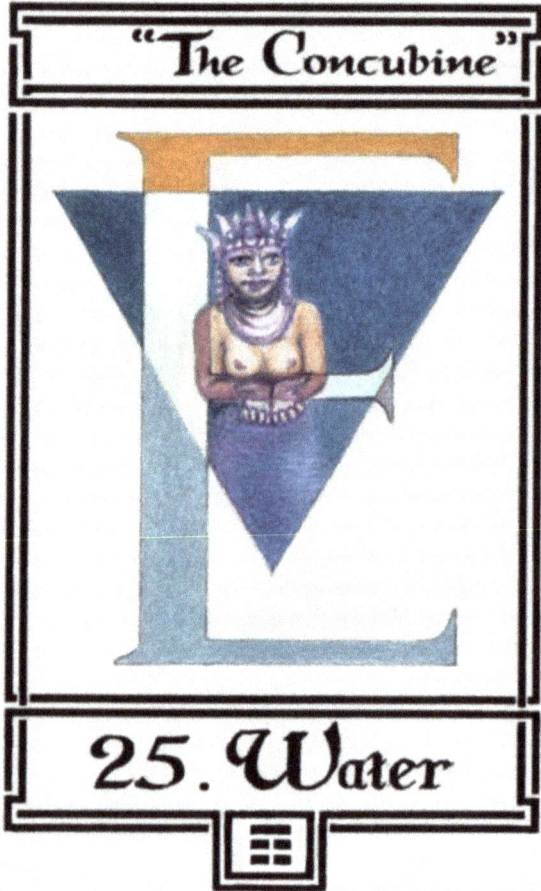

"The Concubine"

25. Water

FINDING NEW SYMBOLS

Hidden passion. Secret romance. Secret affair or affection. A willing slave or servant. Devotion. Dedication. The giving of love. Unconditional love. The giving or receiving of love and emotional strength. The act of charity. A beggar. Actions for love's sake. A helpful person or one who needs help. Aid. Assistance. Entrapment. A victim. A pretence of virtue. Temptation or supplication. Selflessness. A situation or a person with hidden depths. Mysterious motivation.

Liber XXVII: Trigram xxiii. 25=E
"The core of flame, concealed with a crust of earth."
(Life united with Love.)

THE FOOL

FINDING NEW SYMBOLS

A carefree state or person. A guaranteed destination. A glad journey. A new prospect. A wise or a foolish pilgrim. A sense of safety or security which may or may not be justified. Certainty in spite of the unknown. Faith in the present moment. The "light at the end of the tunnel," or a person with confidence in the future. Refusal or inability to learn from mistakes or experience. Folly. Daintiness. Carelessness. Negligence. A person inattentive to their own well-being or future. A person blithely unaware of risk or danger, or who is insured against those. A potential peril or the avoidance of it. Jeopardy.

Liber XXVII: Trigram xxvi. 26=P
"The end is sorrow, and in the sorrow is the Six-fold Star of Glory which shines upon the return to the Stainless Abode."
(All becomes Nothing in the Unity of Love.)

The Trump cards represent different states or situations or environments or people who embody these. The last four Trumps, The Aeon, The Hanged Man, The Concubine, and The Fool, are the four Elements in their purest condition; their presence in a spread will "dignify" any smaller card of the same suit. The suit cards present the dynamic forces of the Elements in their different modes and expressions of manifest activity.

THE SMALL ARCANA

The numbered cards represent the four characteristic types of energy expressed in the Elemental forces, in ten different situations. This is the same model as used in the majority of Tarot and playing card decks, and we saw no reason to alter anything; the progression according to the traditional 10 Sephiroth of the Hebrew Tree is entirely adequate and useful as a descriptive map or template. We have kept our divinatory interpretations of the Small Arcana brief and to the point, as they are necessarily similar to those provided with other esoteric Tarot decks; the reader may note a different emphasis, but the principles being described are more or less the same.

The Wands are the energies used in starting and going forward. The Cups are the energies that nurture and contain. The Swords are the energies that analyse and cut back. The Disks are the energies used in expanding growth and stability.

The Court cards are twelve in number, each suit having a Knight, a Queen, and a Page. They most often indicate the types of individuals who are or will be involved in the matter. The Knights represent the Cardinal qualities in each Element; they are the most dynamic and energised aspects of the Element. The Queens represent the Fixed qualities, the most receptive and magnetic aspects in each Element; and the Pages are the most subject to change, having the Mutable qualities in each Element. The Knights introduce and push forward, the Queens contain and hold, the Pages distribute and disperse. The corresponding Elemental Trump card is the principle source of the power embodied by the Court cards, and if the corresponding Trump appears in the spread the greatest dignity will be conferred upon the Court card. Other cards in the same suit which appear in the spread will similarly be strengthened, and will contribute to and be enhanced by the presence of the Court cards. A predominance or a scarcity of one suit will indicate a general trend in the spread; for example, in a ten or twelve card spread the presence of four or more Disks and an absence of Swords would suggest a bias away from logic and towards consolidation, especially if accompanied by the 24th or the 3rd Trump.

The **Knight of Wands** is a sportsman and a champion, a competitive and forceful leader. Ill-dignified, this headstrong man becomes an oppressive bully.

The **Knight of Cups** is a romantic generous man with artistic sympathies; broad-minded and easy-going. When badly dignified he is immature, selfish, immoral and perverted.

The **Knight of Swords** has a scientific intellect and is a good orator, intelligent and knowledgeable. Ill-dignified, his clever wit becomes sarcastic and cruel.

The **Knight of Disks** is a careful manager, a steadfast man, dutiful and hard-working, a businessman. Badly dignified he becomes dull, pedantic, miserly, and ruthless.

The **Queen of Wands** is an enthusiastic independent woman with nobility and passion, a good friend and hostess. Badly dignified her warm-hearted style is exaggerated and becomes arrogant, bawdy, and vulgar.

The **Queen of Cups** is a caring maternal woman, loving and kind, contemplative and thoughtful. When ill-dignified her capacity for affection is distorted and becomes suffocating, possessive, and hysterical.

The **Queen of Swords** is a dignified and virtuous woman, self disciplined and tactful, with good judgement and clear thought. Ill-dignified, her sincerity becomes hypocritical, deceptive, and she is inclined to be jealous.

The **Queen of Disks** is a busy practical woman, hospitable and hardworking, with determination and ability. Badly dignified she is a shrew; dishonest, vain, and envious.

The **Page of Wands** is an ambitious eager youth, loyal, active, and confident. When ill-dignified the Page's extrovert nature becomes quixotic, rash, and rude.

The **Page of Cups** is gentle and imaginative, a poetic dreamer, a naïve youth. When badly dignified the Page is careless and unreliable, listless and easily influenced.

The **Page of Swords** is an observant youth who is a good communicator and negotiator, a merry chatterbox, a quick thinker. Ill-dignified: a negligent, thoughtless youth, a spy, a sadist.

The **Page of Disks** is a prudent youth who is helpful and adaptable, capable and accommodating. Ill-dignified, the Page becomes lazy, ignorant, introverted, greedy, and even treacherous.

Note: We have followed the traditional genders of the Court Cards for convenience and a little artistic pride – after all, featureless robots would have served the purpose of the images – but the character profiles fit any gendered identity, and the pronouns are merely grammatical devices.

THE FOUR ACES

The Aces represent the purest force of their Element. Two or more Aces in the spread indicate that some of the matter is still in potential and as yet not properly formed, which may make the interpretation difficult to determine with certainty.

Ace of Wands: Opportunity, initiation, inspiration, "the green light". Wasted energy.

Ace of Cups: True love, unconditional devotion, spiritual union, compassion. Disease.

Ace of Swords: Divine justice, karma, swift action, logic. Division.

Ace of Disks: Accumulation, profit, expansion, harvest. Inertia.

The Twos represent the Element's dynamic potential in balanced equilibrium. Two or more Twos in the spread indicate a state of balance in the matter, which may be cooperative or antagonistic, but is unlikely to remain static and unaltered for long.

Two of Wands: The stage of planning, making preparations, "getting one's ducks in a row". Procrastination.

Two of Cups: The stage of mutual harmony, union, love. Uneasiness.

Two of Swords: The stage of negotiation. Discussion. Truce. Stalemate.

Two of Disks: The stage of increasing or decreasing, change, balance. A risk.

The Threes represent the Element in a transitional state between force and form. Two or more Threes in a spread indicate a degree of stability which may tend towards inhibition in the matter.

Three of Wands: The formation of associations, cooperation, teamwork. Disappointment.

Three of Cups: The formation of a harmonious environment, healing, reciprocation. Sensuality.

Three of Swords: The formation of division, sorrow, grief. Isolation.

Three of Disks: The formation of skill, apprenticeship, practice. Mediocrity.

The Fours represent the Element is harmonised stability. Two or more Fours in the spread indicate a degree of structure tending towards expansion in the matter.

Four of Wands: The state of accomplishment. Collective. Embellishment.

Four of Cups: The state of satisfaction. Contentment. Boredom.

Four of Swords: The state of removal. Economy. Avarice.

Four of Disks: The state of maintenance. Inheritance. Insecurity.

The Fives represent the activity of the destabilised Element. Two or more Fives in a spread indicate a warning of unstable and destructive conditions.

Five of Wands: A state of disturbance, interruption, irritation. Contradiction.

Five of Cups: A state of loss, misfortune, ill-treatment. Charity.

Five of Swords: A state of weakness, discord, infamy. Degradation.

Five of Disks: A state of breakdown, trouble, impoverishment. Disorder.

The Four Sixes

The Sixes represent the Element's perfected blueprint for manifestation. Two or more Sixes in a spread indicate that harmonious conditions prevail in the matter.

Six of Wands: A successful achievement. A goal reached. A triumph. Doubt.

Six of Cups: A happy circumstance. A pleasant meeting. A new experience. Renewal.

Six of Swords: A new idea. A journey. Realisation. A confession.

Six of Disks: A gift. A present. Giving and receiving gratification. Envy.

The Four Sevens

The Sevens represent the Element divided by Time. Two or more Sevens indicate a scattering of energy in the matter.

Seven of Wands: having too many challenges at once. Perplexity.

Seven of Cups: having too rich a fantasy. Impermanence.

Seven of Swords: a lack of progress. Quarrelling.

Seven of Disks: a lack of endeavour. Pointless activity.

The Four Eights

The Eights represent the Element defined and re-energised. Two or more Eights indicate a reformation of energy in the matter. Whether this is detrimental or beneficial depends upon other circumstances in the spread.

Eight of Wands: a fresh start.
Eight of Cups: a reassessment.
Eight of Swords: a debate.
Eight of Disks: a commission.

The Nines represent the Element reflected by consciousness. Two or more Nines indicate an unreliable state in parts of the matter.

Nine of Wands: The application of force.
Nine of Cups: The enjoyment of good fortune.
Nine of Swords: The exercise of logic.
Nine of Disks: The contentment of ownership.

The Tens represent the Element manifested in consciousness. Two or more Tens indicate a stage of finalisation in some or all of the matter.

Ten of Wands: An enforced halt.
Ten of Cups: A quest fulfilled.
Ten of Swords: A last word.
Ten of Disks: A change of lifestyle.

PART THREE

AN EXPLANATION OF THE ATTRIBUTIONS OF
LIBER XXVII

ARMED WITH THE proofs of AL II:76 as a template for attributing composite sets of symbolic representations of reality such as are utilised by divinatory systems, we turned our attention to the 27 Yi Ching Trigrams which are given in the text of *Liber Trigrammaton*. This is held to be a Class A document and therefore included in the E. Qaballist's repertoire of symbol-sets and word-lists, and it was an obvious proving ground for our research. This experiment led to the addition of the Trigrams in the design of the Tarot Trumps.

Each Trigram is taken to be a representation of a number in Base 3. Reading from top to bottom, the three levels are quantitively numbered 1, 3, and 9; the different marks represent a zero in the case of the dot, a single unit in the case of the solid line, and the broken line indicates a doubling or multiplication of the quantity by 2. A broken line at the second level indicates the number 6, for example, and at the third level, it means the number 18. The first Trigram therefore maintains its zero state, being composed of three dots.

Of course, these calculations have been used before (most notably by Joel Love) to generate numerical values and discover letter sequences other than the E. Qaballistic order and value of the English Alphabet. We have simply left the numbers generated by the Trigrams as they are and changed the order of the letters. We have not changed the letters "in style or value" but merely altered their "position to one another." The rule of E.Q. is "Follow the numbers!"

Following on from the Zero, the remaining 26 values are therefore attributed to the 26 letters of the English alphabet in the usual E. Qaballistic manner. The letters thus keep their E.Q. values and are presented in a different sequential order. In the first position is the letter K, in the second position is the letter F, in the third is W, and the letter D is the fourth; and so on to the final Trigram and the 26th position which is occupied by the letter P. This Trigram-generated sequence is elucidated by the attributions of the Symbols discussed previously, as the following tables show.

POSITION	TRIGRAM	LETTER &VALUE	SYMBOL
0	● 0 ● +0 ● +0		⊗
1st	● 0 ● +0 ▬ +9	K=9	ꝑ
2nd	● 0 ● +0 ▬ ▬ +(9x2)	F=18	♊
3rd	● 0 ▬ +3 ● +0	W=3	♑
4th	● 0 ▬ ▬ +(3x2) ● +0	D=6	☉
5th	▬ 1 ● +0 ● +0	A=1	♏
6th	▬ ▬ (1x2) ● +0 ● +0	L=2	♐
7th	● 0 ▬ +3 ▬ +9	R=12	♄
8th	● 0 ▬ +3 ▬ ▬ +(9x2)	21=M	♍

TABULATED CORRESPONDENCES OF THE FIRST 9 TRIGRAMS, THE ALPHABET, AND SYMBOLIC ELEMENTS

POSITION	TRIGRAM	LETTER &VALUE	SYMBOL
9th	• 0 ▬ ▬ +(3x2) ▬▬▬ +9	Y=15	〜〜〜
10th	• 0 ▬ ▬ +(3x2) ▬ ▬ +(9x2)	T=24	▽
11th	▬▬▬ 1 • +0 ▬▬▬ +9	V=10	♅
12th	▬▬▬ 1 • +0 ▬ ▬ +(9x2)	Q=19	♋
13th	▬ ▬ (1x2) • +0 ▬▬▬ +9	G=11	♆
14th	▬ ▬ (1x2) • +0 ▬ ▬ +(9x2)	B=20	♌
15th	▬▬▬ 1 ▬▬▬ +3 • +0	H=4	♃
16th	▬▬▬ 1 ▬ ▬ +(3x2) • +0	O=7	♀
17th	▬ ▬ (1x2) ▬▬▬ +3 • +0	S=5	♂

TABULATED CORRESPONDENCES OF THE SECOND 9 TRIGRAMS, THE ALPHABET, AND SYMBOLIC ELEMENTS

POSITION	TRIGRAM	LETTER &VALUE	SYMBOL
18th	(1x2) +(3x2) +0	Z=8	☿
19th	1 +3 +9	C=13	☽
20th	1 +3 +(9x2)	X=22	♎
21st	1 +(3x2) +9	J=16	♈
22nd	(1x2) +3 +9	N=14	♓
23rd	1 +(3x2) +(9x2)	E=25	▽
24th	(1x2) +3 +(9x2)	I=23	△
25th	(1x2) +(3x2) +9	U=17	♉
26th	(1x2) +(3x2) +(9x2)	P=26	⧍

TABULATED CORRESPONDENCES OF THE THIRD 9 TRIGRAMS, THE ALPHABET, AND SYMBOLIC ELEMENTS

The story of the Mutations of the Yin and the Yang can now be read in the sequence of the symbols. It begins with the three forms of Nothing, under which Nothing itself lies. The "Single One" is Pluto, the outer guard and edge of the planetary solar system, and Lord of the Realm of the Dead. (There is a duality implicit in Pluto, who is alive in death, and whose value is the same as FIVE and NINE. NINE=9=K, the first letter in the Trigram sequence, and belonging to Pluto, while FIVE=5 refers to the fifth sequential position, which is symbolised by the Sign of Death, Scorpio, and is occupied by the letter A.) The duality is equilibrated by the Mother who brings forth the Gemini Twins with the letter F in the second position of the sequence indicated by the Trigram values. Thirdly comes Capricorn, the strength and force of "the Demiurge". The Sun naturally formulates the Cross, and Scorpio makes the Imperfection manifest with death. By the alchemy of SAGITTARIUS=146=HEREAFTER and THE WOMAN + STARS the inherent duality of existence is veiled to resemble a single letter, L, in the 6th position of the Trigram sequence. Saturn is the terrible "giant" who appears next, followed by the "Master of the Temple" who embodies the virginal purity of Virgo to accomplish the balancing of everything.

Then we find the first indication of the accuracy of this interpretation, for the ninth position has two Trigrams given in the text, one a reflection of the other in the horizontal plane. The first has the number 15 (=Y), to which is attributed Aquarius, the Zodiac Sign identified by E. Qaballists with Lucifer. The second has the value 7 (=O), to which is attributed Venus, the planet identified as the Morning Star: this is the "confusing of the symbols".

The tenth position is attributed to Earth, which also has the quality of a Water-Bearer (THE STAR=AQUARIUS) and in the text there is a reference to amniotic fluid in the abyss of the Womb. URANUS=66=EARTH reiterates the protection. The next verse mentions APHRODITE (=128) and HERMES (=92) whose combination is (128+92=220 the verses of the Book of the Law), hermaphroditic, and held in open secrecy as the unborn child: the Symbol is naturally that of the Mother, Cancer. Then comes Neptune, the obvious Symbol for work of concealment and treachery. This is followed by Leo, the Sign of pleasure and games, whose shape may be recalling the shape of the lyre; and the next Symbol is JUPITER=143=PERFECT and TERRIBLE. The sensuality of Venus then appears, her spirits travelling upon the lightning flashes in the storm; followed by the fearlessness of Mars, and the destructive logic of Mercury. The Moon is the swaying Heaven. Libra the Scales of Justice and Aries the Babe are the "violent light" and the "soft light" of the Equinoxes. Pisces is naturally the Sign of the "gathering of the waters" preceding the Symbol of Water itself, out of which comes first the "crust of earth" and then the globe and Symbol of Fire. The fire-lighting "upon the earth" is the hierophantic message of Taurus, and the Fool of the Air reveals the way home.

This story, assembled from clues in Liber XXVII and our previous studies of AL II:76, is one in which each episode is foreshadowed by its predecessor and contains the essence of the subsequent event. It is suggestive, but it does not in itself constitute a proof of the proposed attributions. After all, it is quite easy to make a story which links two or more phenomena into a narrative. In fact, a different yet equally consistent narrative may be produced by taking the

Trigram stanzas in the E. Qaballistic Alphabetical order, so that the 5th Trigram (representing the number 1=A), "The Imperfection made manifest" comes first, followed by the 6th (representing 2=L) and the Woman who veils the Upper Heavens. The 3rd (3=W) and the division of purity by the Force of the Demiurge is next, and then the 15th (4=H) with the "Horror of Time", and so on. The sequence ends with the 26th Trigram and the "return to the Stainless Abode."

The proof is obtained when we take the 27 Trigrams to the Complete Tree and use the template of II:76 to plot their positions (see Diagram 4 on page 177). Only the Sphere of Tiphareth in Heaven remains untouched in this schema, for "there are three, and three, and three, and one: and the One is indivisible". This sphere is the eternal and infinite energy substance in which everything manifest and unmanifest always exists, and of which everything manifest and unmanifest is always made. It is, was, and forever will be, the quintessence of all: its number is 113 = SPIRIT, CENTRE, I AM LIFE, etc.

Note that where the Trigram has a reflected form, both Symbols are given, separated by two vertical lines as used by astrologers to indicate a parallel relationship.

The three dots of the zero Trigram are the three veils above Manifest Kether. The Middle Pillar Sephira of Kether, Tiphareth, and Yesod all have Trigrams which are symmetrical on the horizontal axis, while on the Perfect Tree we find that Chokmah, Chesed, Geburah, and Hod also have horizontally symmetrical Trigrams, forming a pleasing harmony; and there is one more in the 93 section. The Key Grapheme G, attributed to Leo, has a Trigram which is the same as its horizontal reflection; this is also confirmed in the value of G=11. These eight spheres have a sanctity of completion within themselves, while the remaining 18 are linked one to another by the reflection of the primary Trigram into the shape of the secondary Trigram. There are also symmetries on both the Manifest and Unmanifest Trees across and diagonally between the "side Pillars".

We have already noted that Pluto the king of the dead and Scorpio the House of Death in the Zodiac are linked by their assigned Trigrams. The connection of the Trigrams attributed to Aquarius and Venus further supports our proposed solution to the problem of placing the letters of the English Alphabet in the context of *Liber XXVII*. The primary Trigram informs the secondary which in turn enhances the primary, thus the Morning Star is informed by the Water-Bearer where WATER=65=A LIGHT, and Venus informs AQUARIUS=THE STAR. Jupiter gives to Saturn with the jollities of saturnalia and receives in return Saturn's permanence into his perfect plan; the Hermit of Virgo is fearless in the encouragement of Mars, whose bold force is equilibrated by purification and isolation. The Trigrams of Sagittarius and Gemini reveal the Art of uniting the divided which is the alchemy of the Twins. The Trigrams of Taurus and Water remind us of the Cup, of the necessary possession of water, and the wisdom of the mother's words transmitted to her offspring. We may even ascribe the three dots of the zero Trigram to the individual human being in the physical pattern of head, torso, and legs; in the three spatial dimensions of the individual's physical being; in the trinity of the individual identity and the perceived material reality and the unseen or occult reality; and so on.

The reflection of the Libra Trigram in the topmost sphere of the Perfect Tree is a reiteration of the total numeric value of the Perfect Tree, LIBRA = 58 = 4+6+3+8+1(=A)+20(=B)+9(=K)   +2+4;   and   the reflection of the Pisces Trigram into the central "O" of MOR (ascribed to Libra) shows why and how the Complete Middle Pillar from Manifest Malkuth to Unmanifest Kether short-circuits at MOR. When the connection is made between Manifest Yesod and Unmanifest Geburah as Malkuth is raised to Da'ath, we find the Babe of Aries prepared for birth through the paired reflections of the Trigrams of Neptune and Cancer. It is the logic of Heaven in Unmanifest Hod that these things should be thus.

Amen.

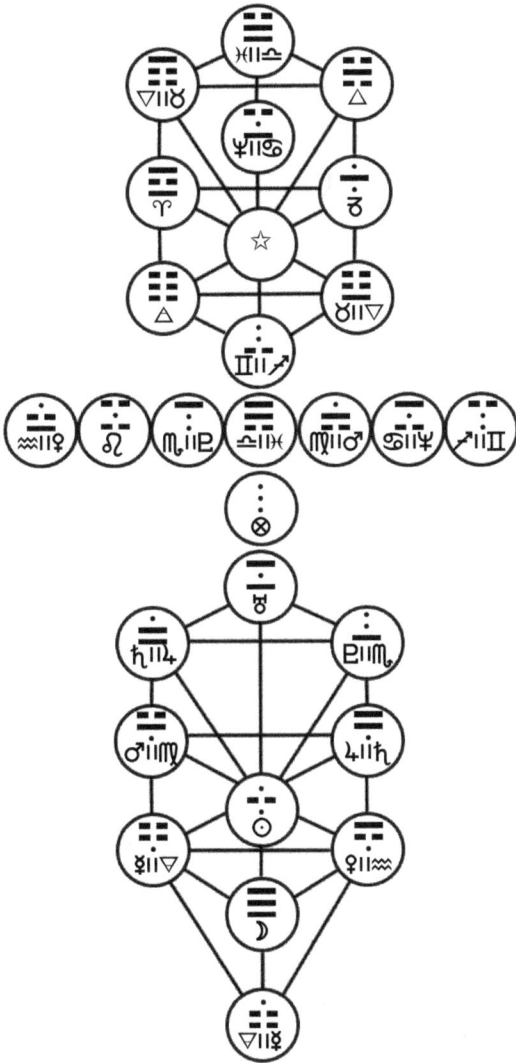

DIAGRAM 4: CORRESPONDENCES OF THE 27 TRIGRAMS ON THE
COMPLETE TREE

PART FOUR

ADDITIONAL REMARKS

THERE FOLLOWS A set of Tables presenting all of the correspondences which have been discussed in this book.

II:76 KEY & VALUE	SYMBOL NAME & VALUE
4 =4	♓ PISCES=97
6 =6	△ FIRE=78
3 =3	▽ WATER=65
8 =8	♑ CAPRICORN=121
A =1	♈ ARIES=66
B =20	☆ SPIRIT=113
K =9	♉ TAURUS=76
2 =2	⊿ AIR=36
4 =4	♊ GEMINI=117
A =1	♆ NEPTUNE=145

1ˢᵀ Whole Tabulation of the Top Tree

NAME in LIBER AL & VALUE	LETTER & VALUE	EQ SUM
RA HOOR KHUT=97	A=1	199
NUIT=78	L=2	164
TA-NECH=81	W=3	152
BES-NA-MAUT=128	H=4	261
RA-HOOR-KHUIT-120	S=5	192
JESUS=68	D=6	207
AHATHOOR=60	O=7	152
RA=13	Z=8	59
HOOR-PAAR-KRAAT=117	K=9	247
HERU-PA-KRAATH=136	V=10	292

II:76 KEY & VALUE	SYMBOL NAME & VALUE
L =2	♒ AQUARIUS=95
G =11	♌ LEO=34
M =21	♏ SCORPIO=93
O =7	♎ LIBRA=58
R =12	♍ VIRGO=63
3 =3	♋ CANCER=78
Y =15	♐ SAGITTARIUS=146
X =22	⊗ WILL=30

1ˢᵀ WHOLE TABULATION OF THE 93 SECTION

NAME in LIBER AL & VALUE	LETTER & VALUE	EQ SUM
KA=10	G=11	118
HRUMACHIS=100	R=12	157
TAHUTI=93	C=13	220
HADIT=58	N=14	137
ISA=29	Y=15	119
KHEPHRA=81	J=16	178
ASAR=19	U=17	197
KHU=30	F=18	100

II:76 KEY & VALUE	SYMBOL NAME & VALUE
24 =24	♅ URANUS=66
89 =89	♇ PLUTO=76
R =12	♄ SATURN=73
P =26	♃ JUPITER=143
S =5	♂ MARS=39
T =24	☉ SUN=36
O =7	♀ VENUS=71
V =10	☿ MERCURY=115
A =1	☽ MOON=49
L =2	▽ EARTH=66

1ˢᵀ WHOLE TABULATION OF THE BOTTOM TREE

FINDING NEW SYMBOLS

NAME in LIBER AL & VALUE	LETTER & VALUE	EQ SUM
HAD=11	Q=19	120
HERU-RA-HA=76	B=20	261
RA-HOOR-KHU=73	M=21	179
MENTU=101	X=22	292
KHABS=39	I=23	106
NU=31	T=24	115
COPH-NIA=88	E=25	191
AIWASS=38	P=26	189
KHONSU=56	----	106
TUM=62	----	130

E.Q. TAROT TITLE	E.Q. TAROT LETTER & VALUE
THE MOON	N=14
THE AEON	I=23
THE CONCUBINE	E=25
THE DEVIL	W=3
THE EMPEROR	J=16
- - -	- - -
THE HIEROPHANT	U=17
THE FOOL	P=26
THE LOVERS	F=18
THE MYSTIC	G=11

2ND WHOLE TABULATION OF THE TOP TREE

II:76 Key & TRIGRAM		LUNAR MANSION TITLE & CONSTELLATION
4	䷗	2 nd Drawing 4° ♓
6	䷏	Pisces 17° ♓
3	䷚	Horns of Aries 0° ♈
8		Belly of Aries 13° ♈
A	䷲	Pleiades 26° ♈
B		Eye or Head of Taurus 9° ♉
K	䷗	Orion's Head 21° ♉
2	䷗	Little Star of Great Light 4° ♊
4		Arm of Gemini 17° ♊
A		Misty or Cloudy 0° ♋

E.Q. TAROT TITLE	E.Q. TAROT LETTER & VALUE
THE STAR	Y=15
STRENGTH	B=20
DEATH	A=1
JUSTICE	X=22
THE HERMIT	M=21
THE CHARIOT	Q=19
ART	L=2
– – –	– – –

2ND WHOLE TABULATION OF THE 93 SECTION

FINDING NEW SYMBOLS

II:76 Key & TRIGRAM	LUNAR MANSION TITLE & CONSTELLATION
L	Eye of the Lion 13° ♋
G	Neck of the Lion 26° ♋
M	Mane 9° ♌
O	Tail 21° ♌
R	Wings of Virgo or Dog Stars 4° ♍
3	Spike of Virgo or Flying Spike 17° ♍
Y	Covered or Covered Flying 0° ♎
X	Horns of Scorpio 13° ♎

E.Q. TAROT TITLE	E.Q. TAROT LETTER & VALUE
THE MAGICIAN	V=10
THE THRESHOLD	K=9
THE WORLD	R=12
THE WHEEL OF FORTUNE	H=4
THE TOWER	S=5
THE SUN	D=6
THE EMPRESS	O=7
THE JUGGLER	Z=8
THE PRIESTESS	C=13
THE EARTH	T=24

2ND WHOLE TABULATION OF THE BOTTOM TREE

II:76 Key & TRIGRAM	LUNAR MANSION TITLE & CONSTELLATION
24	Crown of Scorpio 26° ♎
89	Heart of Scorpio 9° ♏
R	Tail of Scorpio 21° ♏
P	A Beam 4° ♐
S	A Desert 17° ♐
T	Head of Capricorn 0° ♑
O	Swallowing 13° ♑
V	Star of Fortune 26° ♑
A	A Butterfly or Spreading Forth 9° ♒
L	1st Drawing 21° ♒

FINAL REMARKS AND OBSERVATIONS

WE HAVE PROVED our original proposition, that goetic techniques can be applied to the English Qaballa. We have shown, with a simple attribution of the E. Qaballistic Alphabet to the Complete Tree, that the symbolism of AL II:76 can be used to construct rituals as well as sigils. We have presented a new interpretation of the Tarot, combined with a solution to the Trigram correspondences of *Liber XXVII*.

We have presented two different sets of attributions of the 26 letters of the English Alphabet upon the template of the 28 Key Graphemes of AL II:76. Although there are obvious parallels and balances between our fourfold ritual framework and our divinatory system, it is advisable to work each one separately, in its own terms.

The main difference between the divinatory and the ritual format, is that the latter excludes the spheres of Yesod and Malkuth in Manifestation, while of the former, the 26 letters of the Tarot exclude the spheres of Unmanifest Tiphareth and the "X" of the 93 section; the added attribution of the Zero Trigram excludes only the Unmanifest Tiphareth, and sheds a different light upon the "X" of the 93 section. The harmonising and synchronising of a divinatory spread is an act of the operator's Will (at "X" in the 93 Section) through the medium of Life (at Unmanifest Tiphareth). In this context the concepts of Will and Life relate to the individual and to the Cosmic respectively, and are too mobile, flexible, and fluidic to be encapsulated in a single letter-symbol. The Complete Tree symbol in this context is active as a representation of the forces at work in the continuity of existence, dynamic and happening all the time, which are observed at a single moment. The observation is translated in the form and pattern of the divination spread.

In the case of the ritual alphabetical attributions, the symbol of the Complete Tree becomes an inactive representation which may be energised by the physical and metaphysical individuated identities of the operator (Malkuth and Yesod in Manifestation). These personalised fields are far too cosmopolitan to be bound to single linguistic glyphs for purposes of ritual and are more useful when remaining free from such fixed limitations.

In this book we have demonstrated several different magical techniques which endorse the English Qaballa's relevance to the modern occultist; and our exploration of the Complete Tree of Life has produced a thorough re-examination of the tarot. That Book of ancient wisdom which has become a staple of the 'Western Occult Tradition' since Levi and his informed successors made it into a bridge between the supposed condensation of Ancient Egyptian mystery teaching and the Kabbalistic Tree of Life has been extended to incorporate modern reality. The matrix of numeric English language correspondences revealed in *Liber AL vel Legis* and delineated on the 28 spheres of the Complete Tree of Life is a reformation of the occult such as has been applied to almost every other field of human activity and specialised study since World War Two. Incorporating new scientific data and revising old traditions, the English Qaballistic Tarot deck is the most conclusive proof so far that the New Aeon has arrived.

The late Victorian style of the "Occult Revival" has been sidestepped by a new generation. The internal paradigms of magical spiritual philosophies that the

Revivalists wove together in the attempt to build a new Temple no longer manage to uphold nor mediate nor redeem the facts of reality, and occultism seems instead to be approaching a metaphysical vacuum devoid of any sort of unified field theory with which to negotiate between past, present, and future. Such was the paralysis induced by the Revivalist's insistence on making everything fit into the old scheme, that some magicians currently abhor almost every use of occult correspondences, while others firmly believe that no other symbol-set can or should exist. The existence of God and the relevance to modern occultism of proof either way are matters of debate; the difficulties of scientifically proving that consciousness exists are still unsolved. Indeed the poetic language of particle physics is adjacent to the jargon of mystical occultism, and some magicians are rediscovering scientific methodologies.

We have attempted to address some of these deficiencies in this book. Some readers at least may find easier resolutions to awkward problems: we do not seek to teach, but we offer what we have learned for any who would choose to do so.

Let the Rituals be rightly performed with joy and beauty!